God Knows Parenting Is a Wild Ride

God Knows
Parenting
Is a
Wild Ride

9 things to hold on to

Kathy Coffey

SORIN BOOKS   Notre Dame, Indiana

As publisher of the *GOD KNOWS* series, SORIN BOOKS is dedicated
to providing resources to assist readers to enhance their quality of life.
We welcome your comments and suggestions, which may be
conveyed to:

SORIN BOOKS
P.O. Box 1006
Notre Dame, IN 46556-1006
Fax: 1-800-282-5681
e-mail: sorinbk@nd.edu

Scripture quotations used in this text, unless otherwise noted, are
taken from the *New Jerusalem Bible*, copyright © 1985 by Darton,
Longman & Todd, Ltd., and Doubleday, a division of Bantam
Doubleday Dell Publishing Group, Inc. Used with permission of the
publisher.

www.sorinbooks.com

International Standard Book Number: 1-893732-38-X

Cover and text design by Katherine Robinson Coleman.

Cover Photograph © Frank Cezus/Getty Images/FPG.

Printed and bound in the United States of America.

Library of Congress Cataloging-in-Publication Data
Coffey, Kathy.
    God knows parenting is a wild ride : 9 things to hold on to / Kathy
Coffey.
        p. cm. -- (God knows)
    ISBN 1-893732-38-X (pbk.)
    1. Parenting--Religious aspects--Christianity. I. Title. II. Series.
BV4526.3 .C64 2002
248.8'45--dc21
                                                              2002001264
                                                              CIP

CONTENTS

Introduction

During a painful root canal, the new dentist asked the magic question: "You have children?" I grinned around the paraphernalia wedged in my mouth, including both her hands. Through awkwardness and pain, I glowed with bliss.

"Four," I blurted. That's all I could say, but the word was a powerful talisman. I was probably drooling by then, but the thought of my kids buoyed me through the ordeal. While I'll never give up nitrous oxide, memory can sometimes be a stronger balm.

I remember each birth, that first foggy sight of a dark head emerging. After a long labor, the final moments flew, and suddenly in my arms, squirming and damp, was the newest family member. Some parents have the presence of mind to name the child and say hello. I could only cry. That mingling of emotions—pain and ecstasy, relief and fear, joy and dread—pretty much characterizes the next thirty years or so.

At one time we carefully prepared a crib, receiving blankets, tiny sleepers, and a rocking chair. In the years that follow, we still spend time waiting, preparing. Just as we anticipated a daughter or son's birth, so we sit in endless car lines, waiting for one familiar figure to emerge from school or soccer practice. In later years, we cook a favorite dish, make a welcome banner, and put clean sheets on the bed of one returning from college or graduate school, or from a career in another city or travel abroad.

In between the waiting and preparing times come a few spaces for pure enjoyment. One occurred recently at a folksy restaurant, warm with wood and the aroma of scones baking. I have sat around many dining tables with friends my age, savoring their wit, their enthusiasms, their unconscious charm, their individual takes on aging or parenting or politicking or whatever process we're discussing. But this time was different.

The laughter still flowed around the wooden table. Hot coffee kept the conversation bubbling, and each one contributed her unique viewpoint. But the women that day were half my age. After an overnight visit to see my daughter, she'd gathered some friends to have breakfast before we all went to work.

I wish each of their parents had a hidden peephole on the scene, to relish that meal with each delightful daughter. Someone had sacrificed energy, time, and money for the education, the medical care, and the wardrobes they wore so effortlessly today. While a graduation represents a public pinnacle, this was a small and ordinary triumph. Whoever had gotten up in the middle of the night with these lovely young women when they were small and had the flu probably never imagined their beautiful unfolding.

The opportunity made me grateful for the privilege of this window on their lives, for sharing intimately, but at a distance. Where else in human experience do we come so close to a life that is not ours? It's like living immediately, with an extra life, an enhancement. Anyone who has given birth or adopted a daughter or son can call the child "mine, but not mine; intimate, but independent."

In the same paradoxical way, anything we could say about parenting is "true but not true." While some generalizations seem to fit everyone, each relationship nuances the broad strokes differently. Like the stubborn stance of a toddler insisting "mine!", each child's uniqueness challenges anything we could say definitively about everyone. Even within the same family, with the same parents, and in the same environment, the differences among individual siblings are breathtaking.

The God who loves variety had a field day when creating families. Some will thrive on conditions that depress others. One crew won't blink about a situation that causes major upheaval for another. Much as external appearances differ, inner lives—personalities, talents, viewpoints—will be distinct as well. But it only makes the adventure more exciting. Whether you are just beginning to parent or have been parenting for years, welcome aboard. It's a magnificent ride!

About This Book

Reading this book probably won't give you any easy answers or quick gimmicks. Slick promises to "do this and your kid will go to Harvard" are bogus anyway. Given the infinite variety of kids and parenting styles, no one solution could work for everybody. Some of the suggested activities may resonate for you; others may repel.

What this book should give is a new or renewed appreciation for your child and a deeper respect for parenting. Whether your child is long-planned or a surprise, adopted or biological, the first or the third, you sometimes take her for granted. It often takes an outside reminder of how unique and splendid he is. Furthermore, we grow blind to the wonder of parenting. A nudge or reminder helps: as the scriptures say, "that you may know the great hope to which God has called you."

The parenting task you have begun or will soon begin takes all your skills and energies. But it will also be the work of which you are most proud, in many ways the highlight of your life. Compare your time spent on this book to the in-services and updates that guide a career. Few of us would respect a professional who wasn't in touch with the newest thought in the field that energizes and inspires. No one who is successful in a job would try to last for thirty years on the impetus of the original steam. Instead, they refuel periodically for inspiration and new direction. Assuming that parenting isn't all that different, that ongoing update is the goal of this book.

The Author as Parent

I am the mother of four children ages sixteen to twenty-eight. While no longer the parent of young children, I am still very much involved in parenting. One daughter is home full-time, one college-aged son is here for summers and vacations, and the two college graduates visit frequently on weekends. So if there are grammatical errors, cloudy logic or botched syntax, blame the kids' interruptions.

While I'm not still changing diapers, I hope I have gained a perspective now that I lacked from when I did. Time, maturity and skills bring new meaning and appreciation as I look back over those early years. I now know the bottom line that younger parents may still wonder about: *we survived them*. And they survived us.

When the children were younger, I taught English at several Colorado colleges. My present work as author, editor, and retreat director has focused on spirituality. While a Christian perspective has thus influenced my parenting, my children in turn have kept me grounded, never allowing my faith to become airy.

A Faith Perspective

When I try to describe this blend of children and spirituality, I often turn to the scriptures of my Christian faith, one passage in particular from the gospel of Mark:

> People were bringing little children to [Jesus], for him to touch them. The disciples scolded them, but when Jesus saw this he was indignant and said to them, "Let the little children come to me; do not stop them; for it is to such as these that the kingdom of God belongs. In truth I tell you, anyone who does not welcome the kingdom of God like a little child will never enter it." Then he embraced them, laid his hands on them and gave them his blessing.

Forget the Sunday school posters, with the deliberate ethnic balance of cute kids who are dimpled, beribboned, and scrubbed. In this group, as in any group of children, one has a cold, one is cranky because he needs a nap, one has suspicious mucous around the eyes, and an overly eager one elbows Jesus.

The soupy religious art misses the point: the kids are NOT perfect any more than our own offspring are. The loud ones compete for attention and the shy ones hover on the outskirts of the scene, terrified of the stranger.

Jesus scoops the whole kit-n-kaboodle into his wide-flung arms. What he does is an example for all of us. The extent to which we do it shows what kind of human beings we are. The measure of our success in this endeavor is how we welcome the whole noisy, demanding, insecure, rowdy bunch. Including, of course, all our own shadowy, needy, inner children. The ultimate acid bath here is that in rejecting any of this crew, we reject the One who created us.

A good way to reflect on this passage might be to picture our own children, and a few nieces, nephews, and neighbors to fill the open arms. Don't mentally dress them for the occasion or clean up the act. Think of each child in a dirty shirt, telling a long and apparently pointless story. Now the crunch: How can we be any less accepting of children who are like this than the Holy One? How can we not hug them to ourselves? Can we see in them not only our own image, but God's? Even if they unrolled a whole roll of toilet paper. Even if they lost the new jacket. Even if one more interruption will push us to the brink.

On that note, let's turn to *God Knows Parenting Is a Wild Ride.*

Discover Your Partners in Parenting

EFFORTLESSLY,
LOVE FLOWS FROM GOD INTO
HUMANS,
LIKE A BIRD
WHO RIVERS THE AIR
WITHOUT MOVING HER WINGS.

Mechthild of Magdeburg

Ask any parent what they feel when they first see their newborn child, and you'll discover a depth of emotion that words cannot touch.

Nothing before parenthood (getting the lead in the school play, graduating from college with honors, finding a soul-mate and falling in love) or after becoming a parent (a job promotion, an award, a child's wedding or graduation) can quite touch this experience. Perhaps we feel ourselves caught up in what thirteenth-century writer Mechthild describes. We are squarely placed in a flow of love from God to human beings.

With varying degrees of intensity, that channel of grace continues throughout our lives as parents. Sometimes we draw on that strength when we are desperately tired, angry, or ready to strangle our offspring. Sometimes we sense it in joy: a child does something kind or just walks in the door. We know then as we did when we first saw that tiny creature, that we are in way over our heads. Something beyond the human is stirring here, and we want with all our hearts to be a part of it.

Perhaps that is why so many young parents return to a faith tradition cast aside during their adolescent and early adult years. Not only do they want some spiritual foundation for their children, but they want some way to express, deepen, and share this new place where they find themselves.

For they are now in on a well-kept secret. You don't hear much about this secret from religious leaders, or even, unfortunately, from other parents. Maybe it's the kind of garment you grow into, like those slightly-too-big jeans you bought your child because they were on sale. But gradually, over a long experience of parenting, after some sleepless nights and some days that demand the energy of dynamos, you get the larger picture: you aren't in this alone. You and God and other people are all in cahoots.

It's only logical: the monumental task of nurturing a sacred soul, guiding a small person into healthy adulthood couldn't be left to the likes of us. No need here for the whole litany of our failures. Let's just say that humans as a species have some limitations, and parents are no exceptions. Or to paraphrase Paul of Tarsus: We hold a treasure in earthen vessels—the kind that crack and crumble and get stained and dinged—to show that this extraordinary power comes from God and not from us. (For the undiluted version, see 2 Corinthians 4:7.)

This knowledge should bring immense comfort to those who must rely more exclusively on their personal parenting resources than any previous generation. As confidence in institutions erodes and the influence of extended family dwindles, we no longer lean on the support of established customs and traditions. To put it bluntly: Grandma doesn't live with us anymore. Not that this is all bad— sometimes those customs stifled and those traditions restricted. Surely today's diversity is a gift our ancestors didn't enjoy.

As parents, we not only partner with God, but also with other people. Grandparent or godparent, aunt or uncle, adoptive or foster parent, teacher or catechist, neighbor or friend, sibling or mentor—all play a vital role in the life of a child. When asked to identify the most influential person in their faith development, eighty percent of adults name their grandmother.

A nationwide survey of 273,000 young people conducted by the Search Institute identified key building blocks for human development. These assets provide security and give a child a renewable resource. In a society which can be hostile to the young and dangerous to their potential, these elements contribute to healthy and productive lives. Young people having these assets are statistically less likely to engage in problem behaviors such as alcohol use, early sexual experience, school failure, or violence.

Few of us would be surprised that the top three assets are related to parental support and communication. But the fourth-ranked asset is "other adults besides their parents that kids can turn to for advice and support." Of those surveyed, forty-nine percent have this asset: a trusted neighbor, teacher, coach, relative or youth group leader, and ideally, three or more.

Consequently, the Search Institute staff encourages parents to seek out other families and other adults their kids can turn to. They suggest that communities offer mentoring programs and that schools provide personal counseling and faculty support for individual students. They encourage children to call an adult friend when they need advice and to seek out adults who share their passion for things like music, cycling, computers, and hiking. This may sound daunting, but a simple conversation may have positive, long-range effects.

The research only confirms what human beings know instinctively: it's a good thing for the generations to rub shoulders. In a world that tends to segregate by age, young and old need each other. The Hispanic community has always known the importance of the *padrinos*, godparents or "second parents," who remain involved throughout their godchildren's lives.

One intergenerational example comes from a grandmother who voiced her goal for her grandchildren: "I want to give them time to imagine." She explained that contemporary children live structured lives: chauffeured from school to piano practice to soccer to ballet lessons; they rarely have free time. In contrast, she remembered the summers of her childhood, spent outside for long periods of time when cloud-interpretation and clover-chain-weaving were the only items on the agenda. "They need that space," she mused. She also knew such free time was a rarity in a society where the five-year olds carry palm pilots! That then would be her gift to grandchildren: unscheduled time in which to wonder, stare, and think.

Thus the generations gift each other. That grandmother knew that child better than any remote author ever can. Parents can be grateful that others play a tremendous role in their child's growth and development. Celebrate it. Enjoy it. And if you feel isolated, seek out others, in babysitting co-ops, play groups, neighborhood rec centers, retirement homes or churches. Inviting others into your parenting enriches both your child and yourself.

FAITH IS THE WORD THAT
DESCRIBES THE DIRECTION OUR
FEET START MOVING WHEN WE
FIND WE ARE LOVED. FAITH IS
STEPPING OUT INTO THE
UNKNOWN WITH NOTHING TO
GUIDE US BUT A HAND JUST
BEYOND OUR GRASP.

Frederick Buechner

Discover Your Partners in Parenting

- Pause for a moment to see if this notion of partnering in parenthood rings true with your experience. Think about a parenting event that was way beyond you, when you knew for sure that something had surpassed your bleakest flaws. Maybe your child snuggled up and forgave the blunder when you—for perfectly obvious reasons—yelled at her too loudly. Maybe, unasked, he cleared a pathway through his room or she took out a mountain of trash. Or, she was kind. Or, he was creative. (If the pronouns become mind-boggling here, it's an accurate reflection of the amazed-befuddled parental state of mind.) Maybe you got a hint that some seed you had planted so long ago you'd almost forgotten it was sending out the teensiest green shoot.

- If you're brand new at parenting, remember an experience from childhood when your parents surprised you with something wonderful—or you surprised them. Suddenly, they were proud of you, or they expressed a loving emotion you had never heard from them before. Perhaps you rose to an occasion, either helping out in an emergency or celebrating a joy, like baking Mom's birthday cake or achieving a goal in school or sports. Whatever the experience was, pause now to think about it or discuss it with someone else: a spouse, a parent, or a close friend.

- Make a list of the people who helped your parents raise you. Were grandparents, neighbors, aunts, uncles, or friends involved in the process? What exactly did they do? Now list the people you can look to for help during your child's upbringing. What exactly do you hope they will do? Does your support system seem smaller than your parents' network? (If so, that's typical.) If it bothers you that you have few people to turn to, what can you do to enlarge the circle? Have you checked out neighborhood babysitting co-ops? parent groups in local churches or schools? Also note elderly or retired neighbors or other young parents you can turn to. Take an inventory, then make one step this week toward enlarging your support group.

• Through journaling, reflection, or discussion, do some future visioning. How do you see yourself and your child twenty years from now? How have God and other people participated in that process of growth?

• If you haven't already done this, set aside a regular time each day, even if it's just a few minutes, for regular communication with God. This need not be stiff, formal conversation, but the relaxed interchange of friends. For instance, "Sarah's tooth finally came in. Thanks." Or: "I don't know how to pay the bills. Help!" The point is to stay in touch with God.

• If you don't belong to a faith community, visit one church in your area this week. If it makes you want to scream, leave immediately. If, however, you see that it might have potential to enrich you and your child, hang around. See what they might offer.

• Thank someone who helped your parents with your upbringing, or you with your own parenting. A thank-you can take many forms: an e-mail, a phone call, a gift. Promise this person that when your turn comes, you'll return the favor and help another mother or father with their young children.

A MOTHER EXPRESSED HER
GRATITUDE TO THE OTHER KIDS
IN HER SON'S SCHOOL. THE BOY
HAD CANCER, AND RETURNED TO
SCHOOL AFTER A LONG ABSENCE
BALD BECAUSE OF HIS
CHEMOTHERAPY. BUT IN A
PHENOMENON THAT IS BECOMING
INCREASINGLY COMMON, ALL HIS
FRIENDS HAD SHAVED THEIR
HEADS TOO. "THEY COULD NOT
TAKE HIS CANCER, BUT THEY
COULD RELIEVE HIS SHAME."

Mary Fisher

Rain on Vacation

During the days of two-children-in-diapers, when the sheer physical care of infants and toddlers was relentless, I probably sensed dimly that God was part of the scene. After all, I didn't wind up in the loony bin, and they somehow survived the early years. But the awareness of God was pushed aside by more pressing concerns: the demands of feeding, diapering, bathing, clothing, and of course providing the latest up-to-the-minute-mental-stimulation which was deemed required by all the experts in the formative years!

So a sense of perspective emerged only gradually as the children grew older and I became the mature and seasoned (ha!) parent. In one memory coalesces an understanding that took years to develop.

For many months we had been planning a brief Florida vacation, with all the complexities of scheduling that entailed. High expectations colored our autumn as we counted the days 'til our departure in December. We worked hard, saved money, and all the time imagined the reward at the end: a hammock swinging slightly in a sea breeze.

The day before the trip, logistics got complicated by a blizzard at home, road and airport closures, flight rescheduling—the whole messy lot. Consequently, we arrived in Miami after dark and proceeded to the Florida Keys oblivious to any scenery that might have hidden in the shadows. Typical mom-worries kept me up most of that first night. I so wanted the children who had never seen this part of the world to like it as much as I did!

The next morning I woke early and dressed for a walk outside before the offspring woke. It felt strange to don shorts and a T-shirt after the winter blizzard we had driven through the day before. As I fumbled for unfamiliar clothes, the sound of rain distracted me.

The steady downpour prompted my worst imaginings. This wasn't in the plan! Would it rain throughout the trip, naively designed around travel brochures in which the sun shone constantly and the sky was a cloudless blue? Would we be trapped in a too-small hotel room while the beach grew soggy and the pool turned chill? Would all our high hopes vanish in some seasonal glitch, some terrible typhoon? (We writers exaggerate the worst case scenarios, but the tendency IS tied to a vivid imagination.)

I ventured outside when the downpour turned to drizzle. To my astonishment, the pearled sky seemed to be clearing: maybe we weren't socked in for the whole day! As I walked toward the beach, the water was the color of gray flannel, but in spots was turning to the jade I remembered, a color of ocean I have seen nowhere else in the world. What turned out to be a mercifully brief tropical storm had simply intensified the aromas of rain forest and flowers so welcome to the winter-starved.

By the time I reached the hotel dock, the weather had cleared into that unique blend of white-turquoise-aqua cloud, sea, and sky that seemed like a planet away from yesterday's snowscape. A delicate blue heron picked its prim way across a rock. As I walked on, I said, silently and conversationally to God, something like this:

You give us a beautiful world in which to raise our children. Then you join us in this enterprise, a silent and constant companion. And you want their good even more than we do. What a relief to know we're not alone—with endless seas and broad skies as reminders that this is a larger, more benign picture than we could have ever drawn.

The news then is good: we live out of a large and generous soul, a cosmos so vast that scientists are just glimpsing a tiny patch of its creative energies. Weather for the rest of the trip was Florida at its best, and that vacation became an oasis.

The sun will keep coming up, your child will say something that will crack your heart open, a new friend will appear, and you will once again be struck by the unbearable wonder and tenderness of life.

Parenting is a mirror that forces you to look at yourself. If you can learn from what you observe, you just may have a chance to keep growing yourself.

Jon Kabat-Zinn

A Lifetime of Support

Laura and Beth had been friends through high school and college. Beth was an only child, but felt a part of Laura's big, chaotic family.

Naturally shy, Beth learned to hold her own at Laura's dinner table, where stories circulated and sibling rivalry kept everyone alert. Laura's dad introduced Beth to gin-and-tonic on the back porch, a summer ritual. Her mom showed Beth how to bake the best apple pie in town. And the two girls were inseparable.

They were bridesmaids in each other's weddings, and stayed in touch even after they moved to different states. When Beth delivered her first son Jacob, Laura flew to visit with her own one-year-old son. Through that first crazy week at home, Laura was invaluable. She cooked, did laundry, and made sure that Beth got naps. An experienced big sister, Laura introduced the new mom to a whole world of receiving blankets, pacifiers, and snuglis. She taught how to diaper a little boy without getting squirted and what to do with all those mysterious baby gifts. When Beth developed a post-partum fever and infection, Laura drove to doctor appointments and took care of both babies.

Twenty-eight years later, Jacob was starting graduate school in Washington, D.C., and his mom was worried. He had few contacts in the capitol, little income, and no job. Furthermore, during a trip to Guatemala, he'd managed to contract a stubborn case of salmonella. His housemates, engaged in their own careers and study, were too busy to be much help.

When Jacob told his mom about his limited food budget and his Sunday night dinner of peanut-butter sandwiches, she wanted to cry. Feeling young, vulnerable, and weepy herself, Beth phoned Laura to tell her about Jacob's "splurge."

"It's gotten worse," she confided. "To celebrate his first 'A,' he made himself a potato-tuna-rice burrito!"

After a blitz of e-mail between the two, Laura arranged to meet Jacob for dinner while she was in D.C. chaperoning her teenage daughter's field trip to the capitol. She deliberately chose a gourmet restaurant, and insisted on appetizers and dessert along with a huge main course. Meanwhile, her daughter drooled at the "older man" even when Jacob recounted his own cooking fiascoes with glee.

At the end of the evening, Jacob and Laura called Beth. They gave her a glowing description of the shrimp cocktail, grilled salmon, and chocolate mousse. As the conversation closed, Jacob whispered to his mom in awe, "Laura paid for the whole thing!" The bill for dinner was probably more than his food budget for the month.

That evening marked a turning point for both mother and son. Eventually Jacob got over his illness, found a job, made friends, and fit into his new surroundings. Mom stopped worrying about him so much. But all of this came about because Laura had teamed with her friend just as they did when they were in high school, college, and the week the baby was born.

GOD'S GRACE, GIVEN FREELY,
WE DO NOT DESERVE,
BUT WE CAN CHOOSE AT LEAST
TO SEE ITS GHOST
ON EVERY FACE. OH, WE CAN
WISH TO SERVE
EACH OTHER GENTLY AS WE
LIVE, THOUGH LOST.

May Sarton

2

Make Your Home a Sacred Space

THE HIGHER GOAL OF
SPIRITUAL LIVING IS NOT TO
AMASS A WEALTH OF
INFORMATION, BUT TO FACE
SACRED MOMENTS.

Rabbi Abraham Heschel

Quick! Identify the sacred moment:

A. An argument erupts in a teenager's bedroom, where acid rock growls menacingly on the stereo and the floor's surface is buried beneath mounds of clothing, books, CDs and association.

B. Beneath the glow of stained glass windows in a Gothic cathedral, a full-throated choir sings the "Alleluia" chorus which the audience hears in solemnity.

Don't rush to identify either one as holy. Instead, consider the hidden dynamics of both A and B before jumping to a conclusion. Holiness surfaces in unexpected places, and the sacred can visit strange surroundings.

Example A, for instance, might in fact be a long-delayed chance for communication between siblings, or parent and teen might voice expectations of each other that have gone unexpressed. What begins as argument might end in reconciliation (a sacred word!).

Despite all the outward trappings of holiness in example B, the experience might be essentially passive for the assembly, when they daydream about what they'll do when "real" life resumes, after church.

Sometimes we would be well advised to adjust our lenses on family living. Here are some questions that might help:

> Do families recognize the holiness in their homes—or reserve "the sacred" to church?

> Do moms and dads appreciate the profundity of parenting—or assume that grandparents and religious professionals have the corner on holiness?

> And can we blame them for not doing so in a culture that often criticizes the family, rarely reveres them?

While that calls for more work than one chapter or one book can accomplish, this simple exercise may start the ball rolling. Ask children to complete this sentence:

Here's what I like best about our family . . .

A more sophisticated version for parents is:

I see God's presence in our family when . . .

Seeing home as sacred space motivates us to invest our time and energy here. Home is the arena for our most influential work. While we may not always be conscious of its importance, we are planting seed and laying groundwork here—not for a stock portfolio, a building, a project or a book, but for an irreplaceable human being. It is essential to see that home is the place where we most often participate in God's holiness, and bring God's compassion and creativity to our most intimate world.

For families who aren't used to this lens, these examples "prime the pump." They are not all geared to traditional, two-parent families, an increasing minority in our society. They also include examples of failure and disappointment, always a valid part of family experience. A few starters:

- A single mom reminisces as she lights the candles on a child's birthday cake. Each one symbolizes a milestone, a progression from the infant's utter helplessness, to the toddler's first lurching steps, to the driver's license and college graduation. In one lighted circle glows a collection of sacred memories, which vanish as quickly as a breath.

- After a stressful week, the whole family stays in their pajamas until noon on Saturday. No rush, no work. Just blessed relaxing, snuggling, and giggling.

- A parent makes a decision with a child about a situation that concerns them both. It's not always easy, but they weigh alternatives and reach a choice they can live with. Much learning transpires and many values are communicated subtly, without a lecture or any classroom-type paraphernalia.

- A parent who has lost a job and can't pay the mortgage explains to the children: "We may not have a wonderful home. But we'll always be a wonderful family."

- A family member returns after a weekend trip, a summer at camp, or a semester at college. Beneath all the things the traveler has stored up to tell the others runs the unspoken message, "how glad we are to be back together! It's marvelous to adventure, but it's good to be home."

- A parent shares an experience that has always meant a great deal. Maybe it's a favorite city, movie, song, place outdoors, or restaurant. Maybe it's taking daughter to the fishing hole, or cooking chili with son. The object or the place prompts a new level of exchange, saying even to a two-year old: "I want you to know what I love. I want you to share this part of my world."

• At the end of a tough day, the whole family collapses in a big bed and reads a favorite story together.

Maybe adjusting the lens to shed more light on families is a matter of appreciating what we have, not focusing on what we lack. Sure, we fail at times, but we continue in confidence when we build on our strengths. We can also consider the alternatives. What would life be like without our kids?

A concrete answer to that question appears almost every morning outside my front door. Because our home adjoins a park, I often watch joggers run through, graceful and swift. Sometimes I know instinctively which joggers aren't parents. Their running outfits match and are more designer in style than mix and match. There is no jelly stain on their T-shirt. To top off their lithe, slick appearance, they wear gleaming white, expensive tennis shoes. Clearly, their last five paychecks have not gone to finance the "Most Expensive Child" competition among their offspring.

Part of me is envious. But another part of me feels sorry for them. How much they've missed— both positive and negative! One especially important area is how much parenting teaches us about what is holy. It doesn't take the presence of children to make a home holy, but they certainly contribute to our sense that significant things are happening there.

While we are immersed in childrearing it is often hard to see that larger picture. The daily demands of clothing, feeding, and cleaning the offspring can consume almost all our time and energy. At times, it takes every bit of strength we have to remain civil. Looking beyond the immediate need seems like luxury. But then a child says something startling, or we get a good nap, and we see that we're part of something larger than ourselves. The way we parent is making a huge difference in the life of a person who will someday take an important place in this society. Remember the old saw about a teacher affecting eternity, never knowing where his or her influence stops? The same is true for parents too when we begin to see and make our home a sacred space.

EVEN WITH OUR ADVANCED TECHNOLOGY, IT COULD TAKE ANOTHER CENTURY OR TWO TO CONVINCE OUR LEADERS THAT WE DO NOT NEED FAMILIES TO BE CHURCHES AS MUCH AS WE NEED CHURCHES TO BE FAMILIES. TO BE HOLY IS TO BE LIKE GOD AND GOD IS NOT A CHURCH. GOD IS A FAMILY.

Kathleen Chesto

Make Your Home a Sacred Space

- Divide some scratch paper or a computer screen into three columns. In the first, list qualities of people you admire. In the second, list qualities of people you consider good or holy. In the third, list the qualities that make you unique. (For the third column you may wish to create separate pages or separate screens for the unique qualities of different family members.) Afterwards, look for overlap. Are any qualities listed in all three columns? Then discuss or reflect on how you define holiness. Did words like "pious, sweet, virtuous" appear on your list? Could you broaden it to include words like "bold, creative, brilliant, probing, funny, restless, searching"? When you look at your lists again, or discuss them with someone else, do you want to change anything on them? Why or why not?

- Don't wait for the ambulance to arrive (see "A Long Perspective," pages 42-45). Spend some quiet time looking around your living room, family room, bedroom or kitchen—whichever room is the center of your family life. Remember all that's gone on there. After several minutes, make a gesture of blessing over the room and its people: a cross, a circle, a bow to reverence all that has happened there.

- Go from room to room of the house sprinkling each space with water. This ritual symbolizes that all are welcome to enter our doors, and that what we do in this home is a blessing and blessed. If this ritual doesn't fit your religious beliefs or the personality of your family, create your own rituals: symbolic actions that signify that your home is and all who dwell therein are in a sacred space, blessed by the Holy One.

• If our family is sacred, so is everyone else's. Talk with your children about families who have less materially. How can we help? While agencies that help families abound, three possibilities to check out are:

UNICEF, 331 E. 38th St., New York, NY 10016, www.UNICEF.org, intervenes on behalf of the emergency needs of women and children around the world. Buying their artistic cards contributes to children in developing countries.

The Heifer Project, P.O. Box 808, Little Rock, AR 72203, www.heifer.org, provides livestock to families in high poverty areas: purchasing bees, a heifer, a goat, or a rabbit for a poor family appeals to your child's concrete-mindedness.

Christian Foundation for Children and Aging, P.O. Box 805105, Kansas City, MO 64280-5105. Your monthly donation helps educate, feed and clothe the child you "adopt" in another country. The child stays with his or her family, but will mail periodic letters, drawings, and pictures. Post these on the refrigerator to remind the family of their special friend.

- Talk about a family you admire. Each of you can choose a different family or all can focus on the same one. What special qualities distinguish them? Remember: we become what we admire.

IN SPITE OF ALL THE IDEAS AND
TECHNOLOGY AND ATOMS IN
THE WORLD, IT ALL COMES
DOWN TO SHAPING ONE
INDIVIDUAL AT A TIME.

Anonymous

A Wise Investment

"Home" can float because it is not necessarily tied to a place but to people. Even those exiled from their homes by war or another disaster can create a warm sense of belonging if some of the family remains together. This is a story of a home that floated, not from dire necessity, but simply for pleasure.

Every June for forty years, the Miller family went fishing for a week on Bull Shoals Lake in southern Missouri. The family grew from five to twenty-five and from one cabin to seven. Every year Jim Miller, an otherwise thrifty dad, would pay the bill, considering it a wise investment in his family.

A highlight of the trip was always "The Day They Rented the Pontoon." They vaguely thought this might improve their fishing, but mostly they liked the adventure of being out on the vast lake together. One year they ran out of gas and had to paddle back to the dock. Another year a thunderstorm drove them to shelter under a shelf of rock. But the year they remember best was the year they almost sank the pontoon.

It never really dawned on anyone that as the family grew and the children got bigger, it might be time to rent a larger pontoon. So one day with about twenty aboard, the Millers revved the engines and steered merrily toward deep fishing waters. Suddenly a few of the brighter, younger family members noticed the boat was leaning. In a few minutes, everyone saw that lake water was lapping the front deck. So of course all the children rushed forward to see. Then all the mothers rushed forward to grab the children. Then someone noticed that this shifted much of the weight precipitously close to the dipping end. Indeed, the pontoon was sinking.

A few volunteered to jump off and swim and a few others navigated, and eventually the pontoon limped ashore. But that wasn't the end of the story. Indeed, it was just the beginning of the legend. The story was now "How We Almost Sank the Pontoon" and was told and retold—out on the lake late at night, at holiday gatherings, weddings, and birthday parties. The legend even outlived Jim Miller, who died shortly before the family's forty-first trip.

What did the children and grandchildren remember about Jim? In the stories they told at the funeral they didn't spend much time recounting all the days he'd driven to work or volunteered at church. They talked instead about his stock response when anyone asked how he was feeling. Even the week that he died, he'd answer, "Fantastic!"

Jim wasn't lying. Although he knew his prognosis was grim, he felt that he'd received more in life than he'd ever dreamed or imagined. Blessed with a splendid family, he gathered them every year at the lake to celebrate the blessings they'd received. As one teenage grandson recalled in his talk at the funeral, "I remember him holding grandma's hand as they'd walk on the beach together." It wasn't "stagey" or "churchy," just the simple annual joy of coming together gratefully.

Not surprisingly, the rest of the Millers still travel to Bull Shoals every June. The kids wouldn't miss it; the adults never have to insist. All other obligations are gladly set aside for one week. For this family a few rustic cabins and some shining waters are the locus of precious stories. The memories are endless and eternal, worth far more than the cost of the trips. Indeed, Jim Miller had made a wise investment.

Tom Stoble

WHO'S TO CARE ABOUT THEM
IF WE DON'T, WHO?

Tillie Olsen

A Long Perspective

When an elderly gentleman attending a workshop on family spirituality was asked to describe a time that he knew his home was sacred space, he hesitated at first. This was new, unfamiliar territory; his age group had always been taught that the church was the holy ground. Nevertheless he began his story by saying, "This happened 62 years ago, and I don't know if I can talk about it yet.

"When I was ten years old, I started picking up subtle signs that something was wrong. When my dad got home from work, he wouldn't burrow into his newspaper as he almost always did. He started helping with the cooking and sweeping, even cleaning up the kitchen after dinner—something he never did! If he had announced plans to board a rocket ship to outer space, I wouldn't have been more surprised.

"But Mom's behavior was even stranger. I remember the first morning I woke up and she wasn't there with breakfast. Her French toast or fried eggs were as certain as the sun rising. 'Mom?' I called hesitantly, not sure whether to be angry or afraid. All I knew was, I had to shield my little sister from this cataclysmic catastrophe—and she'd be waking soon.

"When Mom appeared, she still wore her robe. Her hair looked tousled, and for the first time I noticed the ashen tones of her skin. As she hugged me, she mumbled some apology for oversleeping but I was too grumpy to hear it. How could she interrupt the routine of my day, which had always run like a well-oiled machine?

"Even worse, she started taking naps. She was asleep when I got home from school, and when I left in the morning. I learned how to make cold cereal for breakfast.

"Mom just went off for more and more tests, and her stays at the hospital began lasting longer—growing from a day or two to more than a week. Dad looked tired and frazzled, but could never explain to us what was going on. In those days, nobody said the word 'cancer.' My aunts brought casseroles and flowers, but I couldn't stand their solicitous looks of pity. I wanted my mom's casseroles, and I wanted everything to be the same as before, the way it was supposed to be. When I tried to ask Mom what was wrong, she'd cry, so I stopped asking. Now that I look back, I guess we took her quiet, behind-the-scenes work for granted.

We just assumed the whole universe ran smoothly, and home clicked along like a little piece of it—the warm background to important things like baseball and science fairs.

"I guess it's amazing that no one told us how sick she was, but that's how it was in those days. I finally realized what was going on one afternoon as I dived into a new comic book after school. The door bell was an unwelcome interruption, but what startled me more was that Dad arrived home about the same time. He'd actually left work early!

"He drove up just as I opened the door to two ambulance drivers wearing white. I squinted at their vehicle in admiration before I realized why they were here. Dad flushed and tried to explain, but he was more intent on ushering them upstairs to Mom's room. I watched, stupefied, as they carried her carefully on a stretcher down the steps.

"Mom reached for my hand and held it tight, but what I remember best was the next few minutes. She asked the drivers to pause there at the foot of the steps before continuing out the front door. For several quiet moments, she gazed at her living room.

"She must have been remembering all that had gone on there: bringing new babies home from the hospital, eating Thanksgiving dinner, arguing, putting up the Christmas tree, paying bills, celebrating birthdays and anniversaries, vacuuming and dusting, joking, laughing, crying, taking pictures before the first day of school, hauling in a new sofa, listening to music, hugging, saying hello and goodbye. It was not a large house, where activities were spread out; instead the living room was the focus of our family's life.

"She knew she wouldn't see it again," concluded the elderly man. "That was the last time we were all together there: Mom, Dad, my sister, and me. And I knew at that moment, our home was holy. Funny thing is, it all happened without a word."

IT TAKES A HEAP OF LIVIN' TO MAKE A HOUSE A HOME.

Edgar Guest

3

Reverence Your Children

BABIES ARE ALWAYS MORE
TROUBLE THAN YOU THOUGHT—
AND MORE WONDERFUL.

Charles Osgood

Face it. Raising kids can be exhausting, mind numbing, draining, expensive, and all-consuming. Had we known what we were getting into—well, let's not go there. The fact is that parents are engaged in one of the most important tasks they will ever do, and it will consume a good bit of their youth and energy. For proof, look at a picture of your parents when you were two, then when you were twenty.

What gets us through? We've already mentioned the support of God and other people. We've reflected on the sacredness of what we do. Let's focus now on that small person who's at the center of it all. Sometimes we parent not out of abstract philosophy, but out of sheer dedication to the child. In short, we're hooked. We never dreamed how life could revolve around one small person, probably weighing less than fifty pounds.

Dorothy Day, the social activist who established the international Catholic Worker soup kitchens for the poor, attributed her whole conversion to the remarkable birth of her daughter Tamar. "No human creature could receive or contain so vast a flood of love and joy as I often felt after the birth of my child," she wrote. "With this came the need to worship, to adore." Day wasn't the first to experience such wonder, such a total turn-around in her life.

When Mary found out she was pregnant with Jesus, she visited an older relative named Elizabeth. The journey there took several days, long enough for the initial shock of the announcement to wear off. She must have had time to think about her baby, because when she arrived, she sang. Her song is named the "*Magnificat*" for its first words, "My soul magnifies the Lord."

Mary's song echoes back in time to another mother named Hannah who, after a long period of infertility, also exulted in discovering she would have a child. It tunnels forward in time to all who find themselves pregnant now—perhaps as surprised as Mary was initially, but in the long run, thrilled.

Mary's song of joy can become ours, and eventually our children's. While she looks back over the long history of her people, she also delights in her own individual life and the marvels

God has done for her. Each of us might write our own *"Magnificat"* when we think of the people, events, and circumstances that combine to make us who we are. How did we happen to find this partner, this job, this house, in this city, with these other people? Some mysterious design is at work here.

Reverencing our own giftedness, we can begin to reverence our children's gifts. After we have thought about the pattern in our own lives, after we have mined for the gold in our own life, we can help our children find it in theirs. Every parent can help a child discover particular talents, abilities, and strengths—not to mention flaws. Each one of us has unique personality types and preferences.

The play of young children gives them the chance to try on various identities: one day, as a firefighter, the next as a mom or dad, the third as an astronaut. We mustn't dismiss this as useless fantasy. This imaginative play opens possibilities and fires energy. While it doesn't necessarily lead to a career, it sends the child an important message: you can be anything.

As children grow older, parents can provide for them opportunities to try everything: a taste of drama lessons, pottery, ice skating, guitar, cooking, or sculpture doesn't mean intensive training or a life-long commitment, but it lets a child know whether to do more. (Such experimentation should not consume major amounts of time and money; see the cautions in Chapter 6, "Buy Experiences for Your Children, Not Things.") Watching people work has also inspired many a budding doctor, artist, teacher, or scientist.

Besides providing opportunities, a parent becomes an expert at encouragement. The Dallas Cowboys cheerleaders pale beside the cheerleading of the parent who says frequently and in varying modes to different children, "You can complete this project. You do have a gift for languages. You are one terrific soccer player! Could you show me how you perform that function on the computer?" While the last request may be driven by the desperation of the technically-impaired, it's a rare perk when a child can show off a skill in real circumstances of genuine need.

One problem with the job of encouragement, which should come so naturally to parents, is that often our children surprise us. When they demonstrate an inclination or a talent that mirrors one of ours, we smile proudly and say modestly, "Just a chip off the old block." But what if their talents are nothing like ours, we barely have the language to compliment them, or we don't value their achievements?

One dad learned more about quantum theory from his science-major daughter than he ever could have dreamt. Hip-hopping kids teach sedentary parents to dance; meat-and-potatoes families learn how to cook vegetarian. Look at parenting as a chance to live another life and enjoy all the possibilities we missed in our own youth.

This doesn't mean projecting all our unfulfilled longings onto our kids. We've seen enough of that at Little League games that were clearly more about the dads and moms than the kids or at weddings where the bride is a stand-in for her mother's long deferred dreams. Reverencing the gifts of our children simply means that life can be rich and full for those who welcome new potential in their children, encourage their talents no matter how bizarre they seem, and never stop learning from the kids.

One of the most poignant scenes in *Fiddler on the Roof* occurs when the townspeople gather around a couple about to be married. The wedding guests sing, "Was this the little boy I carried? Was this the little girl at play? I don't remember growing older; when did they?" As they join in the familiar refrain "Sunrise, Sunset," we realize how quickly time passes, how precious and brief is our time with our children. It makes us want to have every minute count. We do when we reverence our children.

DO YOU KNOW WHO YOU ARE? YOU ARE A MARVEL. YOU ARE UNIQUE. IN ALL THE WORLD THERE IS NO OTHER CHILD EXACTLY LIKE YOU . . . YOU HAVE THE CAPACITY FOR

ANYTHING. YES, YOU ARE A
MARVEL——AND WHEN YOU
GROW UP, CAN YOU THEN HARM
ANOTHER WHO IS LIKE YOU——A
MARVEL? YOU MUST CHERISH
ONE ANOTHER. YOU MUST
WORK, WE ALL MUST WORK TO
MAKE THIS WORLD WORTHY OF
ITS CHILDREN.

Pablo Casals

Reverence Your Children

- If your child is old enough, look together through the photo album, noticing how he or she has grown. Remark on how tiny fingers and toes once were. Comment on the miracle of growth—not only physical, but also the abilities the child has developed: to speak, to walk, to climb. Highlight the latest accomplishments, which the tiny baby in the crib could never do!

- If you haven't done it already, find a place on the wall where you can begin to mark your child's height annually—a concrete reminder of growth that's easy to see and celebrate.

- Tell your child the stories of how you and your spouse met each other, and the child's birth date. Children love stories in which they are the central figures, no matter how many times the tales are repeated.

- Look at a website or book on human anatomy. Marvel at all the complex systems that make up the healthy person.

- If you haven't started one already, begin a journal in which you record your child's sayings and experiences. What a treasure that will be to look back on in the years ahead!

I WILL SPEAK ABOUT THE NEED TO LOVE THE CHILDREN, AND BY THAT I DON'T MEAN INDULGE THEM BUT REALLY TO ADMIT THAT THEY'RE EXACTLY WHAT WE WANTED WHEN WE SAID WE WANTED CHILDREN WHEN WE WERE FIRST MARRIED, WHEN WE WERE FIRST A COMMUNITY, WHEN WE SAID EITHER OPENLY OR IMPLICITLY THAT WE WANTED CHILDREN TO FILL OUR STREETS AND THEIR LAUGHTER TO FILL

OUR EARS. THAT REALLY HASN'T
CHANGED,   BUT   SOMETHING
DOES CHANGE SOMEHOW AND
THAT TENDS TO BE THE ABILITY
TO ADMIT WE FORGOT HOW
IMPORTANT THEY ARE.

Maya Angelou

Stay-at-Home Dad

A dad named Tom sat with a giant green "Moe's Bagels" balloon tied to his finger as we chatted over lunch. His three-year-old son Isaiah played around the perimeter of the table, pausing now and then for a bite of bagel or a swig of juice. Neither dad nor son was conscious of any irony as the balloon swayed overhead and Isaiah swished underfoot in his black super hero cape.

But then, this dad wasn't especially conscious of being radically counter-cultural either. Tom resigned from a teaching career as department chair at a prestigious high school to stay home with Isaiah while his wife Nancy completes her M.D. "After about three months, I figured out that no one was coming to relieve me," he smiles. "When I really settled into the role, it got to be fun. We run through the fountains at the park like kids together.

"People can live on one income, even if it's not very big. If it's at all possible, I really believe one parent should stay home for the first few years." He speaks with pride of his most recent accomplishment. Bear in mind that this man has completed a graduate degree, published successful books, been elected teacher of the year, and addressed a crowd of five thousand at graduation ceremonies. Yet he brags about shopping at Home Depot, with a toddler who needs urgently to use the bathroom, tugging at his feet.

"Home Depot is a guy kind of place," he admits, "I knew I wouldn't get much help." Somehow he maneuvered the bathroom alone, one of the tiny triumphs that constitutes daily life with small children.

Tom's decision to stay home has brought both poignant moments and rewards. In the first category falls a conversation begun when Isaiah asked, "Why is Mommy at work?"

Tom tried to explain, "God gave her a gift to help the sick boys and girls."

Isaiah retorted, "But why? Because I miss her a thousand times!"

Yet Tom and Nancy's decision has not been without its rewards. As father and son sat at the bus stop waiting to go to the opening baseball game of the season, Isaiah at three commented, "Papa, you're my best buddy."

Tom was there when Isaiah saw his first icicle and asked, "Is that a snow worm?" After Tom made a picnic breakfast to share on the bedroom floor, he explained where sausage comes from.

Isaiah promptly said, "Thank you for making us breakfast, Mr. Pig."

"I do all I can to awaken his sense of wonder," says Tom. "I want him to have the poetic gift of noticing everything. We do little rituals together. At bedtime we say our prayers together." And one can imagine the most renowned family experts nodding in approval, saying, "Anything done once with children is a tradition."

Tom has also learned to shift his agenda, to postpone what he wants to do until Isaiah's naptime or bedtime. He recounts a conversation familiar to every mom who's ever tried to take a leisurely bath.

"Are you in the bathroom?" demands a small voice.

"Yes, I'll be out in a minute."

"Well, I'll be in in a minute!" Isaiah replies, barging through the door.

Tom has compiled stories of his son's childhood in *The Salamander Moon Drop Book*, a personal journal with this preface: "I hope we can remember these moments as revelations of God's grace, generosity, and sense of humor. Especially God's sense of humor."

The book contains entries like this one:

> As I was lying in bed with Isaiah I explained, "You know you're very lucky to

have your own bed to sleep in, your own room. Many children in the world don't have a bed or a house. They have to sleep on the ground, sometimes in the cold and rain."

Suddenly Isaiah began to cry and said, "we should go and get them and they can sleep in my bed, and live with us. I can call them my brother and sister."

Reverencing children can be a costly proposition in terms of career advancement. Yet an observer suspects that twenty years from now, Tom probably won't have to join in the familiar refrain, "I wish I'd spent less time on the job, more time with family."

Laurie, Chris, and Isaiah Pramuk

WHEN SOMEONE LOVES YOU, THE WAY THEY SAY YOUR NAME IS DIFFERENT. YOU KNOW THAT YOUR NAME IS SAFE IN THEIR MOUTH.

Anonymous child

"We Shall Bear the Image of the Heavenly One"

Recounted below are short stories of four children to revere.

The small Filippino boy was content to stay in his dad's lap through the first part of the church service. He looked around at the other people in awe, his eyes dark pools. But then he wanted to explore more. As the reader began a scripture passage (from 1 Corinthians), the dad gently lowered the two-year-old from his arms to the floor.

The child took one look at the long aisle stretching before him, summoning to endless, unguessed possibilities. A whole world awaited. His eyes, which had been so expressive before, took on a rich new glow. As he took the first tentative step forward, the reader said loud and clear: "Just as we have borne the image of the earthly one, we shall also bear the image of the heavenly one."

I don't know her name, but the little girl, about five, was my sole companion in a hotel swimming pool. Her father supervised from a distance, but she was utterly self-reliant. She didn't swim much, but she relished the water: swirling it with her arms, sinking into its warmth, making ripples on the surface. As she played, she hummed steadily a little song to herself.

If I would put words to the melody it would say something like this: "I don't need anyone to entertain me. I don't need lots of gimmicks or diversions or even other kids. Right now, I'm happy just being me in the swimming pool." She was self-contained, never whining for attention, never bugging her dad to join her. She simply sang her little song to herself and played. When it was time to go, her dad wrapped her in a beach towel, and she went off without a word of complaint. She left me with a picture of what it means to be truly child-like: serene, unconsciously trusting, playful, humming happily.

Another little girl surprised me on my walk through the park. I must admit I was trying to pick up the pace so I wouldn't look so woefully out of shape compared to those who ran swiftly past me on the jogging path. As I huffed and puffed and wondered if I'd burned off the calories from last night's dessert, I heard her voice. "Hi," she said.

The startling thing was that her voice came from above. It took me a few minutes to figure out that she was perched in a pine tree high above the path. Looking up, all I could see among the branches was long, dark hair and a tiny face. She was maybe nine. I responded in kind: "Hi."

It was hardly a time for lengthy conversation, but her greeting affected the tone of my thoughts as I continued along the path. No longer obsessed with exercise, I remembered what it was like to run outside for the sheer joy of it: released from stuffiness indoors, free of adult agendas, with nothing to do but play in the park until someone called me for supper.

Since I was the kind of little girl who would've been thrilled by a perch in a tree, I wondered what she imagined from her lofty spot. Could be almost anything: the park below might be transformed into dangerous seas through which she sailed her galleon. Or perhaps the park was prairie over which she, the brave pioneer, drove her Conestoga wagon. Her vision may have been colored by what she was reading at the time or what stories intrigued her.

I was honored to be a witness, surprised out of my boring adult reverie into her larger vision. Little girls in trees are an under-appreciated miracle; I'm glad I saw one today.

I never saw her, but I know something of her soul. I was walking down a sidewalk where I saw a familiar sign of spring: hopscotch. But this was no ordinary grid, the boxes outlined with white lines. This hopscotch was done with the soul of an artist. Clearly her interest was more in the embellishment than the game.

The boxes wobbled somewhat and instead of a straight alley, leaned more like the Tower of Pisa. They were outlined in pastel chalk, with heavy use of pink. Around the borders, the artist had really cut loose. Swirls of clouds filled the sidewalk like a baroque ceiling. Flowers flowed down the side of the boxes. It was a scene one would hesitate to jump on.

Somehow I knew instinctively that no boy, interested in getting on with the game, would have drawn such a hopscotch grid. Why would he waste time on decoration when he could be throwing the rock, leaping, arguing about the rules? On the other hand, our anonymous artist was much more interested in what the chalk could do: the medium of color on the canvas of sidewalk.

I hope she guards that bright potential as she grows up, and decorates some other stages. She will make the world more beautiful and enrich the game, a gift the players need more than they know.

YOU CREATED MY INMOST SELF,

KNIT ME TOGETHER IN MY

MOTHER'S WOMB.

FOR SO MANY MARVELS I THANK

YOU;

A WONDER AM I, AND ALL YOUR

WORKS ARE WONDERS.

Psalm 139

4

Protect Your Children, Even as You Encourage Them

HOW OFTEN
HAVE WE BUILT EACH OTHER
AS SHELTERS
AGAINST THE COLD.

Audre Lorde

Much of parents' time and energy in their children's early years goes into protecting them from the obvious physical dangers—electrical outlets, traffic, medicine cabinets, and knives. Consequently we sometimes overlook the subtler dangers. We have them immunized, we warn them about strangers, we provide a healthy diet, but still we are challenged to protect them—sometimes from ourselves.

Because parents live in such intimacy with children, we sometimes fail to see how we can

damage them. Tired or angry, we make the off-
handed comment that wounds. Preoccupied with
work or other concerns, we deny them our time.
Caught up in selfish concerns, we forget that they
need us now; other agendas can wait.

Sometimes we need to nourish ourselves before
we can feed them—literally and emotionally! When
nerves are frazzled and tempers fuming, we simply
need to take five minutes in which to calm down
away from the kids. As we steam through a project
that absolutely must get done, do we stop to ask if
it's really that urgent, and what toll it might take on
those small humans in our care?

Magazine editor and author Tom McGrath says
his family life can sometimes be a game of Hot
Potato. "Instead of a potato, though, we pass
around our anxiety." McGrath goes on:

> I can be guilty of this on occasion. Say I
> come home from work feeling frustrated
> and fearful. I ask my daughter how her
> project is going. She replies that it's
> difficult because the teacher wasn't exactly
> clear on the directions. "Not clear on the
> directions!" I roar, warming up. "What the
> heck am I paying tuition for if they can't
> even get the directions clear? Why I ought
> to call that school and give them a piece of
> my mind!" I say, huffing and puffing. And
> then, "Now, how can I help?" "Gee thanks
> Dad, but I think I'll handle this on my
> own," says my daughter as she slips into

her bedroom and shuts the door solidly behind her.

Pin the anxiety on so-and-so is another family game. If there are money fears or relationship worries or just a low-grade feeling of pervasive shame in the family, it can make the rounds. And sometimes parents, because we have the power, can pass it on and immediately yell, "No tag backs!"

A better approach is to deal with our anxiety off-line, away from the kids. To use stress-reducing techniques—counting to ten, a quick prayer, visiting with friends, a walk, or a bubble bath—before dealing with the kids. (I know this is not always possible! We're talking progress, not perfection on this.)

But the facts are that kids need our non-anxious presence. They grow best when they're not exposed to constant doses of drama and trauma and craziness. Life provides enough stress for healthy growth (we all need some). And a little goes a long way.

Other threats become suddenly real, too. Sometimes we are blindsided by dangers to our children that no one could predict. Parents sending their children to school on April 21, 1999, must have had a thought that had not crossed their minds on April 19. "Will my son or daughter come home?" The Columbine slaying April 20 disrupted our cozy assumptions. After the worst school shooting in U.S. history, fifteen high school students lay dead, twenty-two seriously wounded.

A single mom explained how Columbine and subsequent incidents affected mornings with her young son. "I keep finding ways to make our breakfast last longer," she confessed. As he ran for the school bus, she felt the twinge of fear now common to many parents, "Will I ever see him again?"

The fear may seem exaggerated or paranoid, but as plans for copycat events surfaced around the country and even greater terror struck on September 11, 2001, parents couldn't help wondering if their child's school was next on some killer's list. Add in other threats to the vulnerable child: car accidents, disease, drug and alcohol abuse, and it's enough to paralyze parents—or anyone who safeguards children—with fear.

Cindy Hoffman, an English teacher at Columbine who took a leave of absence after the tragedy, articulated her despair in the newsletter for the Jefferson County Education Association: "On the day my five classes meet again, two faces will be absent. And all of the grief management literature in the world does not prepare me to say to my students, 'I am so passionately, intimately sorry. I will believe forever, in the part of me I can only identify as maternal, that as a teacher I let you down. I could not even keep you safe.'"

We can be vigilant with our children, but even the most protective parent has to let go. Children have to have space, too. They have to make mistakes as they learn life's lessons.

We wish we could weave for our children a protective cape. In fairy tales, the magic cape was often knitted from red wool, made with a generous hood. Sometimes it was silvery or invisible, guarded in a pocket against the moment of necessity. Always, it saved the beloved child from danger. Even to touch it gave the hero a sense of invincibility. "Bring on the worst!" the wearer of the cape could say. "Nothing can defeat me!"

How touchingly simple, we think. At the same time, we long for just such a solution. "If I could give my child an unfailing protection, I would. If I could create for him or her a bullet-proof vest that would ward off all life's dangers, I'd do it in a minute."

Perhaps we can. Perhaps the invisible shield we hang over our children is made up of the values we instill in them, our desperate caring, our prayer for their safety. So we turn to prayer—for our children and maybe just as much for ourselves. We join our concern with God's—the divine parent who loves them even more than we do.

We do not pray for our children in some wishful way, superstitiously trying to prevent all harm. Instead we take an active stance that recognizes our human limitations at the same time it bows before God's power. "I will do everything I can to keep them safe," we say. "But I'm imperfect. I call on you, great God and loving parent, to protect them when I cannot."

This prayer also recognizes the difference between God's ways and our ways. How often we label something "disaster" that instead brings blessing. Ironically, Roberto Benigni, receiving the Academy Award for *Life Is Beautiful* thanked his parents for giving him "the greatest gift of all: poverty."

The Chinese tell the story of a farmer who owned one horse. When it escaped the corral, the neighbors said, "Bad luck."

The man replied, "Who knows?"

When the lost horse returned, leading a herd of wild horses, everyone in the village rejoiced at such good luck. Said the farmer, "Who knows?"

When the farmer's son broke his leg, the neighbors again commiserated. But when the emperor conscripted every young man for the army, the son was rejected as a cripple. Again came the farmer's refrain: "Good event. Bad event. Who knows?"

We may think we can set the perfect course for our own or our children's lives—but God often has something better in mind. That "something better" sometimes involves a loss, a detour, a plot twist that we'd rather avoid. And yet—in that other way lies unguessed grace.

Great gifts sometimes come disguised as disappointments. For example, a parent's worst nightmare might be an injury so serious it leaves a child without an arm or leg. Yet, we watch in awe as single and double amputees, paraplegics, and quadraplegics compete in the Paralympics that follow the Olympics every four years. Interviews with the athletes reveal that sometimes after devastating loss, great strength of character can emerge. Paralympians do the same feats Olympic athletes do, but they make their achievements in pain. Recognizing this, the Olympic athletes gave the Paralympians a standing ovation when both groups visited the White House after their competition in the Sydney 2000 Games.

So our prayer for our children is modified by the knowledge that we don't always know what's best for them. God does. Thus we join our fondest hopes to a divine plan that is certain and sure. We ask for an avalanche of blessings, all the best God has in store for them.

On *The West Wing* television series, Martin Sheen, playing the President of the United States, makes a comment to which every parent can relate. His daughter, now in medical school, lashes out, "I could never make you happy." Some time later, when he has thought out a reply, he answers her: "All you ever had to do to make me happy was just come home at the end of the day." For parents, that is both the hope we cherish and the prayer we speak.

AS THE LITTLE PRINCE DROPPED OFF TO SLEEP, I TOOK HIM IN MY ARMS AND SET OUT WALKING ONCE MORE. I FELT DEEPLY MOVED, AND STIRRED. IT

SEEMED TO ME THAT I WAS
CARRYING A VERY FRAGILE
TREASURE. IT SEEMED TO ME,
EVEN, THAT THERE WAS
NOTHING MORE FRAGILE ON
ALL THE EARTH.

Antoine de Saint-Exupery

Protect Your Children, Even as You Encourage Them

- Discuss with a friend or spouse, or journal about these questions: As you look back over your own life, which apparent disasters turned out to be good in the long run? How does knowing this difference help you see disappointments in your child's life?

- As you are falling asleep, repeat your child's or children's names slowly and reflectively. Ask that the child might be protected and become all he or she was created to be.

- Interview an older person about childrearing, focusing especially on the question: How did you try to protect your children? What qualities of freedom did you try to help them develop?

- Draw or imagine the protective cape you would like to give your child or children. If they are old enough, tell them about it or show them the drawing.

- Think back over your own childhood. What reassured you? What scared you? Then ask your child the same questions. How are the answers different? similar?

- If your child is the right age for it, read together a book about a parent protecting a child, for instance, *A Father Like That* by Charlotte Zolotow or *Hazel's Amazing Mother* by Rosemary Wells.

GRANDMA WAS A KIND OF

FIRST-AID STATION.

Lillian Smith

Anointed

When Julie and Blaine Robb had their youngest son Caleb christened, their attention was focused on keeping their three older boys from total mayhem in the church. All three regarded the long aisles and solemn spaces as runways, perfect for the take-off of their pretend toy airplanes into the soaring Gothic arches. The parents hoped desperately that the "Vroom, Vroom" noises of three toddlers wouldn't drown out the words of the ceremony.

But at some point during the baptism, Caleb was anointed. The oil on his bald forehead bathed him in fragrance and marked him as special. It was accompanied by fervent prayers that he be strengthened as a Christian and protected from harm.

Caleb grew up to be a handful, probably in self-defense. As they raised four boys, Julie and Blaine seldom had time to think back on that baptismal anointing. They spent more time in emergency rooms and on soccer fields, at orthodontists' offices and in teacher conferences than they ever did at church.

But both parents managed to attend the religious ceremony that preceded Caleb's high school service project. His school set aside three weeks of senior year for students to spend in oncology wards and homeless shelters, soup kitchens and retirement centers. Kids who had been somewhat pampered were being called to heroism—they would put their youth, their talents, and their educations at the service of society's needy.

As each student stepped forward, he or she was anointed with that ancient Christian symbol of strengthening. Parents and teachers prayed that students be supported during a difficult time, when they would see more suffering than many of them had ever encountered. When Caleb's turn arrived, Blaine whispered to Julie, "He may not know he needs this now. But in days to come, he'll draw on this deep source."

Blaine's words proved prophetic. The symbol would spiral through Caleb's life again, later that year. A hot-shot skier like his brothers, Caleb made a fatal turn at high speed. He crashed into a tree in an accident so devastating that the Flight for Life helicopter landed directly on the ski slope. Phone calls to his parents warned them he might not survive. Julie phoned their minister as they dashed to the hospital.

The first thing the minister did in the hospital room was anoint Caleb. As Julie and Blaine watched the oil flowing over bandages, they prayed for miraculous healing. Teenagers gathered in the waiting room joined their prayers; they knew their friend was in critical condition. A long ordeal eventually ended. Although Caleb lost an eye, he recovered almost completely. Once again, a blessing and protection of his life had been represented by the symbol of oil.

LETTING GO INVOLVES RADICAL FAITH. IT MEANS ENTRUSTING WHAT YOU MOST LOVE TO THE EXPANSIVE CARE AND PROTECTION OF GOD. BY

THIS I DO NOT MEAN THAT IF
YOU PRAY HARD ENOUGH GOD
WILL KEEP ALL THE AWFUL
THINGS THAT COULD HAPPEN
FROM HAPPENING TO YOUR
CHILD. . . . BUT THAT
SOMEHOW GOD'S PRESENCE IS
AVAILABLE TO US EVEN IN THE
MYSTERIES   OF   HUMAN
SUFFERING AND DEATH.

Wendy Wright

Angels, Quilts, and Thimbles

Sarah Fisher's younger daughter Emily had implored for weeks, "Please mom, come to the program at school on Tuesday!" Sarah stalled, made excuses about the amount of work she had to do on Tuesday, complained that elementary school programs wasted her time, and, as she suspected she would from the start, capitulated.

She found herself seated on a hard and backless bleacher in the gym, wondering why she'd agreed to attend a session on hate crime. Looking at the young students around her, she wondered if this was really necessary—they all looked so innocent. But she did respect the principal, who had welcomed her warmly, and she wondered why Emily was so keen on her coming.

The opening video featured Judy Shepard, the mother of Matthew, a University of Wyoming student who was beaten, tied to a fence, and killed because he was gay. Mrs. Shepard eloquently addressed all parents who worry that their child might evoke violent rage simply because of who he or she is, and educated students who might otherwise act from fear or ignorance.

During Matthew Shepherd's funeral, a second shock wave came from the appearance of minister Fred Phelps. He and his hate-filled band held aloft signs proclaiming Matt was in hell and that AIDS was a punishment for "fags." Furthermore, they threatened that other gay people would meet the same fate if they did not change their lifestyles.

But the good people of Laramie, Wyoming would not allow him the final say. They formed a human corridor to protect the funeral cortege from the sight of such cruelty. One particularly creative group wore angel wings, wreaths and white garments. They said nothing; simply stood guard with their sweeping wings.

As activities for the children continued, Sarah slipped into private thought. It occurred to her that the "angels'" action symbolized what parents do all the time. Those who nurture place themselves between the children and the powers of darkness until they are old enough and strong enough to join the struggle. Parents create for them a safe harbor in which to mature, at the same time modeling what they might someday become. After caring adults have stood against the darkness for an allotted time, the children take their places. It's not a particularly angelic role after all; it's a deeply human one.

Sarah's thoughts turned then to her older daughter Monica. From the time she was tiny, her parents had blessed her with simple words and a gentle touch on her forehead. When she reached second grade, Monica started to bless her parents. If they were tired or sick, she'd remember the ritual before they went to bed, and ended their day with a "God bless."

As Monica's schedule became busier, she would call from a high school activity or party and say, "I'll be late getting home tonight, but I didn't want you going to bed without your blessing!" Sarah always felt warmed by that kind affirmation, but didn't realize fully how much it meant until the summer before Monica left for college.

The college orientation committee wrote the parents of first-year students, explaining that they would display a quilt at the opening event of the year. Each student would be represented by a block on the quilt, all stitched together for the first day. They asked the parents to send a block that best represented their child.

Sarah didn't need to think for long about Monica's block. With the help of a friend who sewed, she set the words of blessing in the center of the panel, then outlined the whole with tiny crosses. It looked lovely when it was done, but more importantly, it stood for Monica: throughout her infancy, childhood, and adolescence, the words of blessing had run like a constant theme.

But the principal's words startled Sarah back to the scene at the school gym. The principal was explaining that a parting gift would be given to all the students. Tying in with Sarah's own musing, the principal explained that this was the same token she had given her son the day after he graduated from college. He was headed to California to pursue the good ol' American dream. Eagerly anticipating her gift, he hoped it was large and financial. Yet she gave him something small, with minimal monetary value.

In a gift box he found a silver thimble. "Fill this with love, care and respect for youself," the mom had said. "Then I'll never have to worry about you." The principal explained that she'd like to give each student the same gift. Students who had worked particularly hard on the hate crime project had been chosen to stand at the doors and distribute a thimble to each child.

Sarah's eyes were misty as she saw Emily stand and proudly carry her basket to the door. Her vision was so blurry she could barely see her daughter as Emily pressed a tiny thimble into her hand. "I want you to have mine, mom. Then I'll never have to worry about you," her younger daughter whispered.

Later that day, Sarah placed her thimble in a place of honor on her desk. She couldn't have said exactly what it represented or why it was so important, but somehow it pointed to the same cycle of protection and care in return, as vivid in Emily's life as it had been in Monica's.

During my piano recital, I was on a stage and scared. I looked at all the people watching me and saw my daddy waving and smiling. He was the only one doing that. I wasn't scared anymore.

Anonymous child

5

Be Ready to Expand Your Own Horizons

TO WELCOME A CHILD IS TO
HAVE YOUR HEART STRETCHED,
MADE CAPABLE OF LOVING IN A
NEW AND UNREPEATABLE WAY.

Wendy Wright

Parents may sometimes feel themselves in the awkward spot that Irish legend attributes to Saint Kevin. Devout followers describe him praying with his arms outstretched in the form of a cross. But because his cell was narrow, one arm stuck out the window. When a blackbird chose the palm of his hand for a nest, it created a quandary for Kevin.

This being the story of a saint, he stuck it out. Kevin kept his hand extended through the window until the eggs hatched and the baby birds flew.

Imaginative sorts like to play with the idea of paralysis setting in, numbness in the arm, and Kevin holding fast.

But it may be a mistake to get caught in the story's charm. Then we risk missing the point: the devotion it takes for anyone to launch anything. Or, given the subject of this book: the unsung heroism of parents who provide the nest until the fledglings fly. Few would name themselves saints, yet many find themselves expanding far beyond capabilities they thought were limited.

It all begins with the purchase of the first maternity slacks. This in itself is a major mental adjustment, because young women consider slacks with elastic waistbands one of the many peculiar habits of older women. Having spent the first quarter-century of her life in jeans, the new mom is somewhat appalled that she must now dress like her grandmother.

It gets worse. Even the most chic maternity fashion cannot disguise the fact that these slacks are made for whales. Girls who weigh in at 110 soaking wet cannot imagine they will ever fit, and when they do, it's cause for major depression. Even, for those given to drama, tears.

Of course the picture changes nine months to a year later—depending on how long it takes to shed the baby weight. Then the maternity slacks provide a good yuck. "Could I really have been that elephantine?" Mom asks in disbelief. She saves the slacks should she ever need to punish her ungrateful offspring with a concrete reminder of "what I went through for you!"

But the elasticity of maternity slacks provides only a dim parable, offers only an obscure glimpse of the changes that occur in the heart. The persons we become under the influence of our children are so different from the young people we once were that meeting ourselves coming down the street, we might be hard to recognize.

The Younger Self meeting the Parent Self might at first be shocked by appearances. Is that drool on the lapel? Why such cheap shoes? And has this poor shmuck lost all sense of color coordination? Younger Self is just on the verge of saying to Parent Self, "you've really let yourself go!"

But then he or she notices the lines around the eyes, the stoop in the shoulders and the intent way we watch a small figure in the distance. All the energy focuses on that child. The body even leans in that direction. And Younger Self shuts up because in that disconcerting second, he or she has had a glimpse of holiness.

True holiness, that is, which would probably never give itself such a high-fallutin' name. We are not talking the kind of syrupy piety that dolls up for church, but screams at the kids to get there on time. We are not talking the airy, distant kind of holiness that flourishes in quiet libraries among adults. We are talking here about the real thing— tested in more furnaces than we care to remember, tried in more acidic baths that we ever thought we could endure.

That elusive kindness we have seen crinkling in Grandma's eyes or bending in Grandpa's stoop starts becoming ours. It's the kind of mystery we could never trace precisely, but we suspect that a big part of our new selves is due to our kids.

The story of the Chavez family is a good illustration of parenting stretching parents way beyond their own horizons. Of course it's not the path for everyone and all kids aren't so gifted. For children with challenges, learning to read or tie a shoe is just as great an achievement, requiring as much or more work. But the story is still inspiring and says something to all parents about the price they pay to help their kids attain the heights. They may sacrifice their own comfort, but they themselves expand in the process.

Elena Chavez's graduation from Harvard marked the fifth in her family. While university administrators say larger groups of siblings have attended the prestigious school, it is hard to imagine a family that worked harder or sacrificed more to do it.

Marty, the oldest asks, "Which came first? That we were talented, or that our parents made an implacable stand that we would have great lives and we would do interesting things and we would contribute to society? I know one thing: my mother's willpower is not subject to the laws of nature."

Any parent would be proud to hear a child describe them this way. But consider what it cost Rose and Ray Chavez. He's a draftsman; she types court documents at home. So there's no surplus money. No television. No vacations. Financial aid helped, but the family house was repeatedly mortgaged. Each night Rose would call the bank to see if checks had cleared.

Being human, they must've wished, now and then, for a nice restaurant dinner without the kids. She must have longed for a new dress—or less frivolously, a new stove. The kids rode the bus to high school; the parents probably drove clunker cars. Yet they moved beyond their personal needs and pleasures. Their achievement outshines the sacrifices.

The Chavezes told their kids they could do anything that wealthier Anglos in their hometown of Albuquerque, New Mexico could do. But in a world where little was expected of Hispanics and nothing was given them, they would simply have to work harder. Indeed, after Harvard, three of the older children earned advanced degrees from Stanford.

Their daughter Andrea comments, "I think what my parents did is basically very entrepreneurial. Without any money and without any premeditation or support, they basically made a bootstrap effort to send five kids to Harvard. We're all conditioned to take the risk and make the investment. If you work hard enough and think hard enough, it cannot fail."

Ask most folks how they got embroiled in choir, coaching soccer or tutoring reading, Scouting or an interest in dinosaurs. "Oh, my kids got me into it!" is often the answer. If it is possible to look helpless and proud at the same time, their shrug and smile convey both. Our kids get us into more than we ever bargained for.

While some older folk always label the younger generation selfish, the label is contradicted by some contemporary actions. Each year, thousands of people run in grueling marathons or walk in less arduous events to raise money for various causes. The AIDS Walk, the Race for the Cure of Breast Cancer, similar efforts for leukemia and MS—these and many more efforts are supported by generous, if more sedentary, friends with checkbooks.

People may not articulate why they spend months in training and sacrifice time and money, which they could legitimately spend on themselves. But part of their motivation is commitment to a human family, which is larger than our immediate circle. When one child is hurting, all are hurting. When one family lives in poverty, all families are diminished. So we sign up for another Read-a-thon, commit to another march, and surrender another Saturday.

The Million Mom March is a dramatic example of how parents in particular get stretched beyond their before-parenting selves. Many mothers have been infuriated that neither state nor federal legislatures have passed stricter measures to control gun violence. They know their children's lives are far more at risk in this country than in other nations, which have passed tough laws. So at various sites around the country, they demonstrated on Mother's Day—a holiday which began, interestingly enough, as an anti-war protest.

In true protest style, they held aloft placards that proclaim the terrible statistic: twelve children a day murdered by guns. They chanted the slogans crucial to any cause that succeeds: "The gun lobby is no match for a million moms." "We love our children more than they love their guns." "Our children are more protected from an aspirin bottle than from a semi-automatic." "Take your gun and go to your room!"

With the gathered support of dads, teenagers, kids in strollers, and grandparents, moms challenged the National Rifle Association and all the other groups that oppose stricter controls on guns. These parents marched, promoted new legislation, and became a voting block because their children's lives are at stake.

"Enough!" roared the assembled mothers, and any candidate who did not take them seriously miscalculated their rage. One mother whose child is threatened is serious enough. But a million of them united confronts the status quo. Parenting can do that—change us, stretch us—all for the sake of our children and their future.

THERE ARE TWO LASTING
BEQUESTS WE CAN GIVE OUR
CHILDREN. ONE IS ROOTS. THE
OTHER IS WINGS.

Hodding Carter, Jr.

Be Ready to Expand Your Own Horizons

- As much as possible, introduce your child to different cultures. Help them understand how other children live, play, eat, and worship, even in their own city or neighborhood. Your library is a rich resource for introducing children to other nationalities and religions. Pluralism and interdependence are facts of life in this century. The sooner children begin to expand their consciousness, the happier they will be—now and in the future. In the process, you'll learn a lot, too.

- Journal or discuss with a friend or spouse: How do you think parenting has expanded you? How are you different now with children than you were two, five, or ten years ago without them? This could take the creative form of a dialogue between your Younger Self and your Parent Self as suggested earlier in this chapter.

- What can you do on a local, national, or international level to make the world better for all its children? Study the issues carefully, consider how much time, talent or treasure you can give now, then act—this month.

- Say St. Francis' Prayer for Peace and teach it to your children. It is a creed for parents, and models a way of life that anyone would be proud to follow:

> Lord, make me an instrument of your peace.
> Where there is hatred, let me sow love;
> Where there is injury, pardon;
> Where there is doubt, faith;
> Where there is despair, hope;
> Where there is darkness, light;
> And where there is sadness, joy.
> Divine Master,
> Grant that I may not so much seek
> To be consoled as to console;
> To be understood as to understand;
> To be loved as to love;
> For it is in giving that we receive;
> It is in pardoning that we are pardoned;
> And it is in dying that we are born to eternal life.

- Observe your own attitudes as you watch the televised news or read the newspaper. Does prejudice creep in? Do you assume that certain ethnic groups will be the criminals and others the heroes? What unconscious biases might we unwittingly convey to our children? How can we broaden our attitudes?

THE MOTHER'S BATTLE FOR HER CHILD . . . NEEDS TO BECOME A COMMON HUMAN BATTLE, WAGED IN LOVE AND IN THE PASSION FOR SURVIVAL.

Adrienne Rich

To Love All Children

Fred was a naval officer in World War II and he hated the Japanese. He and his friend Joe had long stretches for conversation as they crossed the Pacific from San Francisco to Osaka shortly after the bombing of Hiroshima.

"I hope we can go home soon," Fred confided. "My older daughter Tracy was just about to take her first steps when I left for naval training. My wife wrote when her first tooth came in and she said her first word. But I wasn't there—I never got to see her big milestones!

"Then my younger daughter Alison was born right after Pearl Harbor. I feel so bad about missing her birth. Of course I couldn't get leave—the country was under siege! They were rushing us off to war. So I've never seen anything but pictures of Alison. I've never held her, never gotten up in the middle of the night when she was crying. It probably sounds crazy, but I blame the Japanese for missing the childhood of my kids."

Joe tried to persuade Fred to join him ashore when their ship finally docked in the Japanese port. "I told you. I'm bitter. I want nothing to do with these people. They took away chances I can never replace, time with my kids I can never have again. I don't want to see Osaka. I just want to see Omaha," he sulked.

But the two officers stayed on deck and watched the activity in the harbor. Suddenly Fred grabbed the binoculars from Joe and directed them toward a small scow.

"Oh no! Look at that! They're harvesting the sewage!" Fred pointed to an elderly man and two children in the choppy waters below. Indeed, Fred was right. Two dark heads gleamed like polished ebony beside the bent figure of their grandfather. With long sticks, the trio combed the seaweed and refuse as though it were the ordinary routine of checking the aisles at the grocery store. They'd retrieve a fish head here, a discarded crust there.

Seagulls screamed overhead, jealous that humans were pre-empting their feast.

Fred went on, outraged, "Those kids are just a bit older than my little girls! C'mon, Joe. We're raiding the commissary."

With most of the crew taking shore leave, no one was around to object. Fred and Joe quickly filled a basket with cereal, bread, fruit, canned soup. Then the two friends motioned to the scow, which approached with some trepidation. Carefully, Fred lowered the food overboard to a grateful grandfather. Sign language carried the message: eat. Enjoy. We are no longer enemies.

Many years later, Fred would tell Tracy and Alison's children the story. He especially liked to recount the tale at Thanksgiving or Christmas, when a fruit basket made the centerpiece for the family dinner table. Fred would hold an orange reverently and talk about how a little girl's dark eyes lit up as she held hers in the boat.

"That little mite," he'd remember. "She probably hadn't eaten one in years—if ever. Right there, despite the waves, her grandfather with shaking hands split it open. He broke it into segments and she shared it with her sister. I'll always remember the look on her face.

"I dunno." Fred shrugged. "Thinking of your mom, feeding those kids—somehow it got harder to hate."

WHAT'S DONE TO CHILDREN,
THEY WILL DO TO SOCIETY.

Karl Menninger

A Second Chance at the Summit

I was a klutzy child. Shy, introverted, and awkward, I detested sports. When the report card arrived, the only problematic area was always the same: gym. It probably tested the compassion of the coach to award me a quarterly "D." I guess I was the last to be chosen for any team because I'd run away when I saw the ball coming. Hitting a volleyball created a nasty crimson welt down one's arm and catching a baseball squarely in the mitt meant a stinging in the palm. Running sweatily down a field after a hockey ball made one's side hurt. Why bother?

Not that it didn't matter to most of my friends. They'd spend long hours early in the morning and late at night practicing. "Team spirit" was the code for their highest value. A humid dressing room or a basketball court blasted by icy winds was their idea of a posh resort. They regarded me with pity. Clearly I was not a "team player" and would never go anywhere in life. They didn't expect me to show up at any class reunions. Due to my pathetic lack of athletic ability, I'd probably spend those breathless weekends in the hospital or at the fat farm.

A brief flurry of an attempt at athletics punctuated the college years. Faced with the dreadful prospect of a spring break spent in the dorms, someone suggested we try skiing. I fantasized snowy peaks against cobalt skies and rum toddies before a roaring fire, cute mittens, and even cuter ski instructors. The fantasies were cozy enough to prompt a down payment for the trip.

I had conveniently forgotten my utter lack of any physical skills. But I was reminded with the directness of the first frigid gust down the slope. After a few practice runs on level ground, the instructor cheerily assumed we'd ride the lift up the mountain, jump breezily off and ski down a bunny hill. The reality struck as I approached the top. "I will either die by jumping off or by continuing to ride through the machinery," I muttered to myself. "And of the two, I'll take my chances with the nasty cog wheels."

The lift operators who appeared comatose sprang into action when one occupied chair went past the jump-off point. They yelled, they waved, they pointed out the obvious. "Jump!" When that failed, they stopped the lift and hauled this incredibly stupid person down. Dumb enough to repeat the scenario, they saw her coming and stopped the lift. Amid much grumbling, they allowed her to clamber off with great fuss and bother.

Needless to say, I retreated quickly to the rum toddy after a couple attempts. How could I have forgotten the "Ds" of childhood? How could I have ever presumed I was anything but a klutz? It was back to the books for the next twenty years.

Then I had kids. Kids who in their sweet innocence knew nothing of the shameful report cards. Kids who assumed Mom could do anything. Kids who wanted to play tennis and swim and canoe and ski. Especially ski. Somewhere during the years of paralysis, I'd moved to Colorado. And that is how kids in the Rocky Mountains spend the winter. As even a klutz knows, kids cannot be disappointed. Or put another way, moms can't take the whining forever.

Besides, I could brightly sign them up for lessons, bundle them off to the slopes, and reappear at three o'clock. No more anguish or ordeal—it was possible to have the best of both worlds! I'd smile as they pulled on their equipment and provide the hot chocolate at the end of the day. How hard could this be?

Except I hadn't bargained on the nagging little voice that wanted to join them. Why let the kids have all the fun? Something in me rebelled against joining the faithful company of moms who sat in the lodge all day reading romance novels. Outside was the heart-stopping scenery of the high country.

People who looked even less able than I (if that is possible) swished down snowy paths with ease.

So I trooped along with the four-year-olds for a lesson. Something about the kids' encouragement got me over the first hurdle: the lift. Could anyone resist a little mitt placed trustingly in mine? "Whee!" I lied, "Won't it be fun to jump off?" And it wasn't so bad. The crisp fragrance of pine, the lure of beauty, the reassuring rhythm of turns through snow that on the best days was like ice cream—gradually, it overcame my neurosis.

The kids did their part too, probably because my funding was crucial to the operation. Clinging to my poles, bent over to watch my feet, proceeding at an ant's pace, I must have been a hilarious sight to other skiers. But not to my kids. "Wow—were you in the Olympics?" they'd call as they whizzed past. "Have you been skiing since you were a baby?" It would take a colder heart than mine to ignore such encouragement. I'd follow a bobbing red cap down the mountain, and go back for more. The kids soon moved on to black diamond runs and complex maneuvers. I'm still cruising the easy trails, soaking in the beauty, humming to myself.

After fourteen years, I actually look forward to winter. The relatives have gotten used to sunny pictures on the Christmas card of us posed at some dizzying height, brandishing our poles. I attend school reunions because revenge is sweet. Is that the star of the basketball team with the raspy voice and the smoker's cough? Does the captain who never chose me seem slightly pudgy and envious as she looks at my photos of skiing? "Gee, I've never tried it," she confesses. "You must have courage." "Nah," I smile modestly. "I have kids."

IN THE EFFORT TO GIVE GOOD AND COMFORTING ANSWERS TO THE YOUNG QUESTIONERS WHOM WE LOVE, WE VERY OFTEN ARRIVE AT GOOD AND COMFORTING ANSWERS FOR OURSELVES.

Ruth Goode

6

Buy Experiences for Your Children, Not Things

EVERY SOUL NEEDS A WALK IN
THE PARK AT LEAST ONCE A
WEEK.

William J. O'Malley

What are your memories of childhood? Put your mental processes on rewind for a few minutes and look back over the highlights.

After you've savored some memories, try to sort them out. Are they mostly about people or things? Places or activities?

An object like a favorite fire truck or doll may have surfaced in your memories, or a place like a vacation cabin. But some of the memories people treasure most from their childhood are those of adults spending time with us. Perhaps an uncle took us fishing, or a grandmother let us help bake or garden. Maybe busy parents set aside their own projects to help with homework or baseball practice.

With many constraints on their time, parents today name their greatest dilemma as wanting to be with their children while also needing to meet many other demands in the workplace and home. From the children's standpoint, surveys show they never get enough adult time! Probably each person works out an individual solution to that stress, learning what corners to cut and what sacrifices to make. As we perform that balancing act, it might help to consider the question: What will your child remember, looking back as an adult on his or her childhood?

As you engage in making your child's memories now, here's one helpful guideline. Given a choice, go for experiences instead of things. Many people will cringe as they read that line, fearing that the experience requires a greater time expenditure. A thing, goes this reasoning, can be quickly purchased and will then entertain the child while we get back to what we'd rather do.

One flaw in the argument surfaces a day or two after Christmas. By then the toys that looked so appealing under the tree have lost some of their luster. Some are broken. Others simply didn't provide all the "fun" promised on the box. One or two will be "keepers," which a child treasures for years. But too many will wind up in garage sales that summer. Then parents will wonder if it was really worth all the overtime they worked to buy the stuff. For a moment, they're weary of the process English poet Wordsworth named "getting and spending."

But then the new catalogues appear in the fall, and the ads hype something the kids can't live without, and the cycle starts again. Children are a vulnerable audience, and marketing is slick. Study after study has concluded that outside of school, most American children watch more television— three or four hours per day—than participating in any other activity except sleeping. One estimate is that they view 30,000 TV commercials each year.

Are we trapped in a pattern we can't break? Who's in charge here?

Probably few of us are so pure that we will never set foot in a shopping mall. Now and then we'll cave in to advertising pressure or novelty and buy something we probably don't really need. But we can take control over crazy spending, and substitute something our kids want more: ourselves, our time.

Sure we're tired. We may groan inwardly at finding more time when we already feel sandwiched. But how often will this child be this little? In a few years, the pestering will stop. He'll be off with his friends, or she'll decide she can't be caught dead with mom or dad. The social mavens of the junior high will rule that someone seen with their parents resides on the social level of pond scum.

Regrets then will be painful to bear. Hence, the following completely debatable Nutshell Guide for What Kind of Experiences to Pursue:

- almost anything outdoors

- unstructured fun—every activity doesn't require a league and by-laws

- intergenerational—the activity gathers folks of all ages around a common interest

- something new and untried that will broaden the horizons

- something familiar and predictable that will sink roots in security.

Each individual and family will have their own (probably quirky) sense of what is fun. So a list won't fit everyone, but here are some prompts to get started:

- sailing

- play dough

- sculpting

- bread baking

- music making

- some sport about which you're mildly fanatic

- cycling

- exploring different cultures

- reading aloud

- board game nights (choose games based on the ages and interests of your family).

Some activities won't fit your style or will seem so hokey you'll never repeat them. Others will become cherished family habits. Either way—how will you know unless you've tried?

Add in a few ritual observances, using "ritual" in the broad sense, because they give children (and frazzled parents) the peace and security of familiarity. For example, on the first day of spring, we always hunt violets. On the Fourth of July, we always eat fried chicken and ice cream. On Labor Day, we always hike. For the first snowfall, we always have hot chocolate, and at Thanksgiving we help serve dinner at Salvation Army, and so on. Adults weary of too many decisions will find with relief that some of them are already made when seasonal customs are established.

What things to avoid buying? A perennial test of a toy is, *who does the work*: the toy or the child? If it's a high tech contraption with elaborate bells and whistles designed to impress, the child is likely to get bored watching gizmos perform. Yet children can dig happily in a sand pile for hours, because their imaginations are active. Without elaborate equipment, they can create roads, cities, dungeons, and towers. They can be equally inventive with a few cardboard boxes and some blank paper. All the electronic toys in the world are poor substitutes for a blanket draped across a table.

In the early years, provide a wealth of different materials for children to try out: drums, feathers, tubs of soapy water, pine cones, blocks, and art supplies. Then watch carefully as your child's unique interests and talents begin to emerge. If he is drawn to music or art, support that inclination early. Ditto if she is drawn to a doctor kit or erector set. Keep the spirit of play—it doesn't mean she'll be a concert pianist, but maybe she'll be an attorney whose musical hobby relieves the stress of a busy career.

High on the list of things to ban is the television. Research more extensive than this book shows the destructive influence of television on children. One indicator: children watching television have the same brain waves as children on sedatives. While there may be times we wish they were on sedatives, and a few times when TV is justified, it is dangerous for its passivity, its violence, and its advertising.

One guideline helped me with my four children: *If they weren't watching TV, what else would they be doing?* The answer can unlock a storm of creativity. Don't assume the only answer is, "They'd be sitting around getting bored and whining." Think instead of the physical exercise they could be getting outdoors, the experiences with reading, music, and art. Think how that passivity could be replaced by the activity for which their healthy, growing bodies were intended. Finally, consider the number of couch potatoes in the United States, and the high percentage of people who are overweight. Do we want our kids to join that population?

Most importantly, who do you want to socialize your child—a human being or an appliance? If that's not enough of a case against the tube, the statistics on violence should speak for themselves. A child by the end of elementary school will have watched 8,000 murders and 100,000 other acts of violence on TV, said a 1992 report of the American Psychological Association. By the age of eighteen those numbers double. The more "real life" the violence portrayed, the greater the chance that it will be "learned."

Furthermore, parents are the last line of defense against slick marketing aimed at children. The marketing appeal is not only geared toward present consumption. Companies hope that brand loyalty created in childhood will last a lifetime. As early as age two, before most of them recognize their own names, children can recognize a brand logo. The attempts of federal agencies to ban television advertising that exploits children's trust and gullibility have largely failed. Madison Avenue is quite aware that working parents who feel guilty spending time away from their children will spend more money on them. Their interest in children's advertising began during the 1980s, when market researchers began organizing focus groups for two and three-year olds. It's enough to make you wrap your child in a favorite blanket, snuggle up together, and read *Goodnight Moon* for the thirty-seventh time.

A special word about eating meals together. If you've noticed that much healthy family life revolves around eating together, you're right. Furthermore, your instinct is supported by research. Surveys done by the National Center on

Addiction and Substance Abuse show that the more often a family has dinner together, the less likely a teenager is to smoke, drink, and use drugs. Children in families that dine together only once a week are more than twice as likely as those who dine together nightly to smoke, drink, and use drugs. If your children are small, set the pattern now: each night you have dinner together reduces the children's risk of substance abuse later in life.

Families with difficult schedules have become creative: one dad who traveled a lot met his wife and kids at the Dallas airport for dinner. Other families have substituted breakfast or a snack before bed together for the shared suppertime.

In general, the experiences to seek out for sharing with your children are those that will feed the soul, tap the human potential, awaken parts of ourselves that haven't yet awakened, and celebrate the beauty of being human.

THE AIM OF MOST CHILDREN'S ADVERTISING IS STRAIGHTFORWARD: GET KIDS TO NAG THEIR PARENTS AND NAG THEM WELL.

Eric Schlosser

Buy Experiences for Your Children, Not Things

- Ask everyone in the family to complete the sentence: "Remember the time we . . . ?" After everyone has a chance, talk or journal about your stories in light of Mary Pipher's description of stories in her book *The Shelter of Each Other*: "Stories reveal what a family wants to believe about itself. They say something about the family, about its character, history and virtues." She subdivides the genre into vacation-disaster stories ("told and retold with more zeal than the disaster-free stories"), cautionary tales, and legends of family heroes. The stories "can transcend time and distance, poverty, and ill health. These metaphors of food, places, trips, beloved objects and beloved people become the connecting tissue of the family." Also, answer these questions: Why are *things* so notably absent from the list above? What does this suggest about priorities?

- Reread a children's classic like *Little House on the Prairie* or *Sounder*. How do families with few things nevertheless have extraordinary closeness and happiness? What do you envy about their lifestyle? What could you replicate?

- Give some weekend time to exploration. Family members can take turns choosing and lead the "voyage of discovery" to: a new park, a new restaurant, a new neighborhood, or a new activity. Compare notes afterward: Do you want to repeat the experience or not?

• If a special event like a birthday or holiday is coming up, ask your child: how would you most like to spend two or three hours together? The answers may surprise you, but try to honor at least one request.

YOUR CHILDREN NEED YOUR PRESENCE MORE THAN YOUR PRESENTS.

Jesse Jackson

Sharing a Full Circle Experience

Rarely does an experience dovetail so perfectly with history, but it happened for one mom and son.

Liz Martin had saved every extra penny for several years to pay for a dream vacation She and her seven-year-old Jeff would spend two weeks in Australia.

Before she left, Liz had lunch with her dad, who had served as a naval officer during World War II. Anticipating her visit to the Great Barrier Reef off the Australian coast, he told her a story of the reef during the war.

He was the gunnery officer on a transport ship, carrying soldiers to Asia. As they approached the Australian coast, the radio officer handed him an urgent message. A Japanese submarine had been detected following their ship. They immediately set a zigzag course to deter attack and began battle preparations. A Dutch officer on board showered, shaved, and changed into a clean uniform—their custom when they prepared to die.

Liz's dad, thirty years old at the time, spent a sleepless night knowing that the defense of the ship was largely in his inexperienced hands. But in the morning, he saw "one of the most beautiful sights of his life." On the horizon loomed a gray Australian destroyer. This ship guided his through the Great Barrier Reef to safety. The passage was so tricky that no one but Australians would know it, and no Japanese would attempt to follow. "And that," concluded Liz's dad in his gifted storytelling style, "was how the Great Barrier Reef saved my life—and the lives of thousands of others."

Liz saved the story like a precious jewel for the precise moment when she would tell it to Jeff. That time came on Heron Island, surrounded by the reef, an excellent site for snorkeling. They were eating lunch with growing excitement because that afternoon, they had booked a trip to a prime snorkeling location. After she told his grandfather's experience with the reef to Jeff, his eyes glowed. "That's an amazing story," he breathed.

Later they launched from the boat into another world. Resting their foreheads on the Pacific, they put all their attention into becoming a Big Eye. They swam above cathedrals and canyons, cauliflower and forests, plates and branches of coral. The fish that swam alongside shimmered in green-blue-gold-like mosaics. Giant silvery ones, tiny black and white striped ones, mammoth turtles all accompanied them. Vistas opened in the purple and pink coral like views of the Grand Canyon.

The experience brought them wonder and delight, but it had an added dimension. Mother and son were both aware that the Great Barrier Reef was not only a place of sublime beauty. Caught up in a story that began before they were born and would continue after their deaths, they felt like citizens of a larger universe. They also knew in some sense, they owed their lives to the Reef.

TEN THOUSAND FLOWERS IN SPRING, THE MOON IN AUTUMN, A COOL BREEZE IN SUMMER, SNOW IN WINTER. IF YOUR MIND ISN'T CLOUDED BY UNNECESSARY THINGS, THIS IS THE BEST SEASON OF YOUR LIFE.

Wu-Men

Moon Lake With Daddy

I sat vigil by my dad's deathbed. The clock flashed 11:15 as I powered off my laptop computer. Outside the darkness turned the window into a mirror. I stared out only to see myself reflected there—and my father lying comatose in the hospital bed.

I didn't want to leave him just yet. I wanted to be with him when he died, but his passing might come in minutes or hours—maybe even days. I had grown too tired to work anymore, though I had an imminent deadline. Ironically, or maybe fortuitously, I was editing a book on grief and loss.

My family has customarily gathered after a relative's funeral to reminisce. As I sat in the stiff chair looking at my dad struggle to take each breath, I began that inevitable process of sorting through what I really wanted to say about my father. That he was a naval officer in the Pacific? That he would have been proud that Kansas State finally had a good football team? That his enlistment in Officer Candidate School prevented him from being on the team that developed the atom bomb? No. That wasn't my dad. Not really.

I surely didn't want to talk about all those years he felt a failure at a job too small for his intellect and skills. The anguish over money and the lack thereof. Not that. As I looked into my dad's eyes, my favorite memory overtook me.

Our fishing trips—just Dad and me (though as a southern boy it was always "Daddy")—started Friday night as we loaded the old Nash with cane poles and gear and hooked up our second-hand trailer on which rode our second-hand boat. No matter. To me they were the best. Then to bed because we would rise long before the sun rose.

We would creep out of the house and be on Highway 51, heading out of Memphis. The streets lay empty before us. The only sounds were the old Nash's engine, the cooing of the doves, and the frantic chirping of invisible birds.

Out of the city we went south into the Mississippi Delta, passing lightening cotton fields and groves of loblolly pines, kudzu covering everything else. Often we'd stop at some small café for grits, country bacon, and sunnyside up eggs, with toast on the side. By then the sun was peeking over the tree line.

Our trip ended at Moon Lake, an expansive slough of the Mississippi River, filled with bluegill, sunfish, catfish, crappie, and enormous gar. By the time we had the boat in the water, the sun was ten degrees off the water. The temperature was edging up. As the old motor coughed awake, Daddy would direct me to shove off. I always felt a thrill as he turned the boat out toward the farther shore, and we glided across the smooth lake.

All morning we fished near shore, in inlets filled with cypress knees and fallen logs. My job was to bait the hooks with minnows or worms, and sometimes crickets or cockroaches we'd caught in traps in our basement. Dad chose the best spots and ran the boat. Sometimes we'd catch stringers of fish, and sometimes we got skunked. Somehow looking back, I never really remember much about how many or how big. I only remember the pure pleasure of being with my dad, out on the water, listening to him tell me about growing up in St. Joe, Missouri, rabbit hunting with Uncle Charlie and eccentric Joe Pfeiffer, or living in the dorm at K-State.

By noon, the fish had stopped biting. The sun made the metal boat's surfaces sizzle. And we were both hungry for the bologna sandwiches that Mom had made for us. So we'd pull the boat under some cypresses, tie up on a handy branch, open the cooler, and take our leisure. Just in case, we kept our poles in the water. Mostly we simply sat in silence—comfortable and easy.

We might keep trying for more catches, but by mid-afternoon we were usually done. Too hot for the fish and too hot for us, we needed a swim. Dad would find a hidden, shaded inlet, then study the horizons for other boats. If the coast was clear, we'd both chuck down to our boxer shorts and ease over the sides of the boat into the muddy water.

I don't think I ever saw my dad happier than he was then, swimming around on his back making sounds like a delirious seal, then flipping over and over, and eventually doing his best crawl in imitation of Johnny Weismuller, my favorite Tarzan. Then he'd grab me and toss me into the air so I could splash and protest. And always he would let me climb on his shoulders and dive in—over and over. Sometimes we'd grab our poles and wade among the cypress knees, pretend-fishing, though we mostly wanted to stay in the water and out of our clothes.

By late afternoon we were back on the road home to Memphis. Inevitably I dozed on and off until we hit the city limits. In those sleepier times, Saturday traffic was still light. The sawing of cicadas greeted us enthusiastically but, as we drove down Central Avenue, blocks from home, I could see my Dad's face begin to tighten again and his shoulders slump. Even so, for those hours in the Delta, Dad was free of his troubles and so was I. We were a boy and his Daddy out on our own, carefree and bathed by the sun.

I looked over at my dad—my daddy—now eighty-five years old, but soon to pass on. I was forty-nine, but those memories were still the best for me. Even when my father finally found professional success and could buy me better than the second-hand Schwinns that I got as a kid, I still most savored those trips to Moon Lake. Dad and I didn't need toys or things to mediate our affection for one another, although I'm not sure he ever quite knew that, and I grew into adulthood before I understood it.

As I thought again about what I would say in our family recollections, I knew that I wouldn't tell this story. It was just too tender. I wanted it to stay between Dad and me. Besides, my Mom would be embarrassed about the image of Dad and I swimming nearly naked out in public.

Almost at midnight, my Dad took his last breaths. Moments before I had leaned over his bed, kissed his forehead, and prayed Psalm 23. I like to think of my Dad sitting down to a heavenly banquet of deep-fried catfish that we had caught just that day, piping hot cornbread smothered in syrup, fresh butter beans, and a slice of rhubarb pie. I think he would be as happy to be resting by Moon Lake as restful waters. I like to remember him that way.

Carl Koch

LOVE MAY BE ENCODED AS CAMPING, BAKING, MAKING MUSIC, SEWING OR BARBECUING. THEY ARE ALL FAMILY PRAYERS.

Mary Pipher

7

Remember That Communication's a Two-Way Street

MAX: "MOMMY, WHAT MEANS
DISOBEDIENT?"
MOM: "IT MEANS THAT YOU'RE
NOT LISTENING TO MOMMY."
MAX: "JUST LIKE PAPA DOES?"

A conversation heard at home

Sometimes dramatic circumstances can reveal the dynamics of communication better than more ordinary, ho-hum situations. This chapter ends on the ordinary note of fruit salad, but begins in jail.

Operation Bedtime Story is a movement that is catching on nationally. This effort tries to strengthen connections between young children and their parents who are incarcerated. The process is simple. An inmate who's a mom or dad reads a story or for a longer book, a chapter into a tape recorder. He or she adds a personal message, then the book and tape are sent to the child or children. The child, enchanted by the parent's voice, can play the tape endlessly and read the book over and over. Of course it's not the ideal connection, lacking the parent's touch and physical presence. But under the circumstances, it may be the next best thing.

This program helps parent and child bond despite prolonged absence. It attunes the child to the joys of reading and reassures that even though Mom or Dad can't be there physically, they're at least thinking of them. But no rationale speaks as loudly as Tandy's voice on the tape: "Dasheta and Annika, I'm going to read you a story. I love you so much and I really miss you. (Her voice quavers with intense feeling.) Listen to this before you go to bed, close your eyes and pretend we're sitting on the couch together, and your mama will be right there with you." One would guess that two little girls drifted off more happily and slept more deeply the nights they played their tape from Mom.

Expand this cameo to all communication between parent and child: Is communication not the thread that connects, the bond that holds us close? Because our verbal and non-verbal ties are so precious, we treat them with the utmost care.

Plenty of books on communication tell us how to be direct and simple in our requests, to say "yes" when we mean "yes" and "no" when we mean "no." They explain that we should look directly into each other's eyes when we speak or listen, and that we should be sensitive to the way non-verbal signals communicate. But like anything else, communication gets interesting when we move beyond the textbook and into the realities.

We discover right off the bat that communication with each particular child is unique—unlike anything the books warned us about (including, of course, this book). But it seems safe to say that like everything else in parenting, certain parameters are set early in childhood. This is how we speak to each other: gently. Respectfully. If we get angry and shout, we apologize later. Every soft-spoken mother of a bossy loudmouth is wondering where she went wrong, but we are talking here not about specifics, but about a general tone. Any human parent is guaranteed to fall short of the ideal.

However, better than using the harsh language of demand, from early childhood on, we can try to frame our requests to our children in the tentative language of mutuality. "Please" softens "pick up your toys!" or "Go to bed!" "Maybe I could help you with that big job" makes it less onerous. If everything we tell our children is a non-negotiable "must do" it keeps our communication on the hard, brittle shell of reality. Phrasing with courtesy and humor has a better chance of penetrating to the core self, the truer identity for both parties.

Robert McClory, a journalism professor at Northwestern University, writes that long before he heard Jesus' words, "you are worth more than many sparrows" or even knew who Jesus was, he understood the message. "I knew I was worth more than many sparrows. The message is conveyed from the moment of birth—mediated in the sights and sounds and touches that the baby experiences without comprehending in its mind what they mean. Yet the message is sealed in the soul: You are important, you are welcome, you are loved."

It's a pretty safe bet that conversations with young children can get repetitive and frustrating. You may replay the same version of a current fantasy or a Disney flick 'til your head aches. But squint at that yammering child for a minute and consider: Do you want the channels still flowing at ages fourteen or sixteen? It's hard to turn on the conversational faucet then if the well runs dry now.

Think of these early conversations as postcards to your children. A parent who travels a lot searches for ways to reassure a child, "no matter where I am, I carry you in my heart." Stay-at-home parents take the cue: Seek every chance to tell that child he's a treasure, she's a gift. Amazingly, a day arrives when parents start getting postcards back: a gluey concoction of popsicle sticks, a birthday card, and eventually, a meaningful phone call from a young adult. The long patient road has become a two-way street.

That road isn't completely uphill. Along it are scattered unexpected delights. For instance, conversations with children take on the added thrill of not knowing exactly who's who. Adults pretty much stay the same; children can go rapidly from being Buzz Lightyear to a burrowing rabbit to good ol' Sam. Three-year-old Ryan tells his mom he can't finish getting dressed because "superheroes don't wear shoes; they just wear socks." But when they are playing in the hot tub together, and mom asks if he will save her like a superhero, Ryan responds, "I'm not a super hero; I'm just a three-year-old!"

We can also learn from our kids. Staring up at the sky one night, a dad asks his young son, "Why is the moon lit up? Do you think it's made of cheese?" The wise toddler replies, "No, the moon is lit up from the sun shining on its reflection."

Children awaken a sense of play in tired adults. After a bath, one toddler invited her parents, "Come in here and watch. It's a game called running around in circles naked." The surprise of the totally unexpected keeps parents on their toes. A mom asking her son, "What do you say when you fart?" doesn't anticipate his answer, "Amen."

For a while the fad was T-shirts that proclaimed, "Treat me no differently than you would the queen." It might not be a bad idea to make those in infant sizes. When we think of the potential ahead, we could aim to use our kindest voices and our finest listening skills. In this communication, there is a lot at stake.

A LITTLE GIRL SUDDENLY
NOTICED THAT HER MOTHER
HAD SEVERAL STRANDS OF
WHITE HAIR ON HER BRUNETTE
HEAD. SHE ASKED, "WHY ARE
SOME HAIRS WHITE, MOM?"
HER MOTHER REPLIED, "EVERY
TIME YOU DO SOMETHING
WRONG AND MAKE ME
UNHAPPY, ONE OF MY HAIRS
TURNS WHITE."
THE LITTLE GIRL THOUGHT
ABOUT THIS FOR A WHILE, THEN
ASKED, "MAMA, WHY ARE ALL
OF GRANDMA'S HAIRS WHITE?"

Anonymous

Remember That Communication's a Two-Way Street

- Spend at least twenty minutes each night reading aloud to or with your child. If you must be away, utilize a tape recorder for a story, or telephone with a briefer message. Silent reading together as a family can continue as the children get older.

- To stimulate conversation, turn off the television and radio. If this feels too drastic, start with one evening a week that is TV-free or one car ride a day without the radio. Watch the conversation blossom, or enjoy the silence together. Religiously preserve mealtime as a no-television-zone. Use these as conversation starters with older kids:

  - "My favorite time together was . . ."
  - "My worst time with the family was . . ."
  - "The thing I would most like to change about our family is . . . "
  - "Here's what our family looks like in 5 years . . . in 10 . . . in 15 . . ."

- For a whole week give one compliment a day to your child. Be sneaky and sincere so the child won't catch on. If it seems to help, repeat the compliments the next week . . . and the next.

- Refrain from comparisons. Avoid "my child is talking before the neighbor's child," "my niece crawled before my daughter did," and "Sarah is much taller than Nicki was at that age." Comparisons imply judgments, a sure-fire way to squelch the unique blossoming of any child.

A LITTLE GIRL APPROACHED THE ALTAR WHERE THE CHILDREN WERE GATHERING FOR THE CHILDREN'S SERMON. SHE WAS WEARING A BEAUTIFUL DRESS, SO THE PASTOR LEANED OVER AND SAID TO THE GIRL, "THAT IS A PRETTY DRESS. IS IT YOUR EASTER DRESS?"

"YES," SHE REPLIED DIRECTLY INTO THE PASTOR'S CLIP-ON MIKE. "AND MY MOM SAYS IT'S A BITCH TO IRON."

Anonymous

Fruit Salad

Few books on communication mention fruit salad—but how much comes together over that bowl!

It's a snowy Saturday afternoon, I've just gotten back from the grocery store, and my daughter and I decide to make fruit salad for dinner. The roads are icy; the wind is chill; it's cozy in the kitchen.

Sometimes in mid-winter when the ground is white, the trees are stark silhouettes and the skies are pewter-toned, we long for color. And here on the table it abounds: green and purple grapes, red apples, yellow bananas, ruby grapefruit, oranges and blueberries. It may be wintry in our part of the world, but in the tropics, flowers bloom and fruits ripen.

Beyond aesthetic appeal, there's taste. We sample freely as we work. Tart and sweet flavors blend; crisp and soft textures meld. I've been reading (probably too much) lately about the dark side of the American diet. Most of us know that we consume too much fat and sugar, too many empty calories. Yet here is genuine nourishment for body and soul—fruit is low-cholesterol food we don't need to feel too guilty about.

An easy conversation flows over the peeling and chopping. "So how was driver's ed. this morning?" I ask tentatively.

"Boring. The policeman talked about train wrecks, and the car dealer told us how to buy a car."

"I didn't know train wrecks were such a problem."

"You wouldn't believe how many people die in them every year!"

"Does the car dealer think you'll be a customer soon?"

"Nah, I think he just wants us to remember Burt's Chevrolet when the time comes. At least we know the right questions to ask."

"How's Andy?" I ask about a little boy she babysits who's been hospitalized with persistent upper respiratory problems.

"Still in the hospital. His mom and dad take turns spending the night there."

"They must be pooped!"

"Yeah. The dad didn't believe how noisy it was until he took his turn. Karen told him over and over, but nope, he had to be there!"

"It's been over a week now. That's a long ordeal."

"Could we send them some fruit salad?"

"That's a great idea—we've got plenty. Might cheer them up. Dig out one of those big plastic bowls with a lid."

"Can you drive me to the school play tonight?"

"Yeah. We picking up any pals?"

"Addie, maybe. I'll call Molly, see who else is going."

"Okay, let me know what time."

I've read that communication with teenagers goes better when we're both absorbed in a common activity. The worst nightmare for both parent and child is grimly sitting down and confronting each other about a topic that must be loaded to demand such serious attention. On a ski lift or in the car, we chat easily. Forced into two straight chairs, our words dry up.

Each grape I drop into the bowl reminds me of an essay I read recently, where the writer was asked, "What is the most important spiritual question of our time?" She replied, "How to nurture good grapes?"

She went on to explain that God relishes particularity: this mountain (Horeb), this person (Matthew or Joanna), or this place (Cana).

Those who grow grapes know that each variety is different: a particular soil, exposure, and climate affects the unique taste. The vintner knows how different flavors complement each other and blend in the wine's bouquet.

So there is also no one perfect template for human beings. A marvelous variety makes the wine of God's reign. A salad or stew would be bland with only one kind of fruit or vegetable. But the coming together of unique flavors and textures makes a delicious dish. So our children will often surprise us with something we might never do or say. But each person's uniqueness makes the composite that is a family unlike any other family.

In some ways, our fruit salad was so ordinary. It was something anyone could create, given a good produce section and a little time. Yet we felt like a fictional character of Wendell Berry's who was "living and working at the center of a wonderful provisioning."

As we ate, we were nurtured in a way that a great dollop of abstract verbiage seldom gives. Words are fine forms of communication, but sometimes an experience far surpasses them.

Something symbolic lingered over that fruit salad, I mused as I dumped the peels in the compost heap. This summer the apple cores and orange peels will feed the green beans and lettuce. It's harder to see nature's cycle with a child. But what we plant in their youth must somehow flower in their adulthood. So we try to guide their tastes towards good things and hope they will value a nurturing conversation as much as we do.

IF YOU WISH TO KEEP COMMUNICATIONS WITH YOUR CHILDREN OPEN, YOU'LL NEED TO STOP INTERRUPTIVE BEHAVIORS, HURRIED PROBLEM-SOLVING, AND DENIALS AND DEFENSES; THEN LISTEN WITH A MIND QUIET ENOUGH TO HEAR YOUR CHILD DEEPLY.

Bobbie Sandoz

Chile, Burritos, and Communication

If the seeds of good parent-child communication are sown early and often throughout childhood, they sometimes flower in adulthood. Parents are often surprised to find that when they reach old age, their children nurture them with the same storytelling and praise they once gave the little ones.

The sign recently went down on Chavez Mexican Food, which had stood on the same corner in Denver for twenty-seven years, and the name of the new restaurant went up. Few people knew the family story behind the change. But the saga began in Mexico when Dolores and Charles Chavez married. Some years later, they spotted an old restaurant for sale. Soon everything clicked, and they were the new owners.

"The first day," one son recalls, "Mom passed out in the kitchen. It was too hot in there. I remember thinking, if we make it through this day, we're gonna make it."

They did—through lots of ups and downs, fights, hard work, success and a gradual slowing of business. By then Charles was in his 80s and Dolores in her 70s.

Somehow customers didn't recognize the huge difference between a drive-through at Taco Bell and beans that had simmered all night. They didn't realize that Dolores' *chile rellenos* were a work of art, and that a *burrito grande* was worth waiting for.

The whole family was getting tired. They invested too much time and energy for too little return. So they made a difficult decision together. While they would always relish Dolores' enchiladas, guacamole, and fajitas at home, they could no longer maintain a restaurant.

"The night we closed," remembers another son, Lewis, "we called it the Last Supper. That was our life. We didn't just work there. Every time we'd walk in we'd say, 'I'm home.'"

There followed a period of mourning and withdrawal. Dolores used to call the restaurant before she went to sleep just to make sure everything was okay. "Now," she says, "I want to call the restaurant, and it's not there."

And because they are the children of Dolores and Charles Chavez, because they grew up believing in duty and responsibility and loyalty, her sons shield her now. If her children could take her sadness from her and carry it in their own hearts, they would. When she is ready they will tease her about the tattooed bikers who towered over her and called her Mama. They will remind her what it was like in summer when Elitch's Amusement Park was in full swing. The park's theater crowd jammed the restaurant, and they could hear the kids screaming on the roller coaster and smell the popcorn and cotton candy, the beauty of what Lewis calls, "the sweet and the warm and the night." They will talk about all the famous people who ate her green chile.

They'll tell her stories until her pain is eased and her heart is warm and full because she is their mother, and they are her children, and this is what families do.

PRAISE YOUTH AND IT WILL
BLOSSOM.

Irish Saying

8

Lighten Up

WHEN MY WIFE QUIT WORK TO
TAKE CARE OF OUR NEW BABY
DAUGHTER, COUNTLESS HOURS
OF PEEK-A-BOO AND OTHER
GAMES SLOWLY TOOK THEIR
TOLL. ONE EVENING SHE
SMACKED HER BARE TOES ON
THE CORNER OF A DRESSER AND
GRABBING HER FOOT, SANK TO
THE FLOOR. I RUSHED TO HER
SIDE AND ASKED WHERE IT HURT.
SHE LOOKED AT ME THROUGH
TEAR-FILLED EYES AND
MANAGED TO MOAN, "IT'S THE
PIGGY THAT ATE ROAST BEEF."

Anonymous

One under-appreciated benefit of life with kids is humor. Of course there are plenty of grim times, tough challenges, and serious responsibilities. But offsetting all those are the crazy times, the bubbling or rumbling laughter, the lightness, and joy that children bring. When we get too solemn, they tickle a nerve or make a face or say something that makes us howl with delight.

In living with children we discover a paradox: lightening up really deepens us. Abandoning "official" roles restores the most important ones.

In the early years, kids' humor tends towards the scatological variety, and almost every parent can describe the pre-school carpool with its preference for potty jokes. But parents who persist through this stage, surrounding their children with good humor, will someday welcome the emergence of a more sophisticated wit. Their children will, consciously or not, diffuse the tensest situations and bring laughter to places where we never thought we'd smile.

Humor is subjective and what regales one will leave another cold. But a take-it-easy attitude provides a healthy atmosphere in which kids can grow and parents can relax. By this point in the book, parents know that everything they do is safely nested in the larger realm of God's hands. To some extent, that's freeing. Not that we totally abandon our commitments, but we see them within a bigger framework that enables us to laugh now and then.

Given a society plagued by stress, it becomes almost a counter-cultural statement when parents go easy—on themselves and their children. The pressures on kids have been well publicized, but those struck forcefully when I mentioned during a workshop that parents didn't *have* to sign up their kids for every imaginable activity. A genuinely concerned dad interrupted to ask, "But if we don't, won't they be behind the other kids?"

"How old are your children?" I asked.

"Three and five," he answered.

I wanted to free him from the burden of getting them into Harvard right now. I wanted those parents to tear up the tight schedule of ballet, Little League, music lessons, drama, soccer, and art class. I wanted their kids to splash in a backyard pool in July, make snow angels in January, take some cozy naps, and smell the rain. I wanted to yell, "Run! Break free of all the expectations! And take your kids with you!"

Which of course I couldn't do, and he probably couldn't do completely. But we can all find the cracks in our days where the grace seeps through. For ourselves and our children, we can concentrate less on achieving, more on being happy. Sometimes we are so full of tension, there's no room for God. And that is being entirely too full of ourselves.

Magazine editor Tom McGrath tells this story on the website "Weekly Meditation for Busy Parents" where you can sign on for a brief meditation that arrives hassle-free via e-mail every Monday (www.homefaith.com):

When I was about ten, our old car died. My parents took my older brother and me along to shop for a new one. We knew we should buy another old clunker, but there was this brand-new, shiny, turquoise Chevy Impala, fully loaded, very sleek. My parents warned us solemnly that if we bought this car we would have to scrimp and save. We begged them to buy the car. There would be no more extra treats in the grocery cart, and we certainly couldn't be going out to dinner. "We understand," said Pat and I. We were willing to sacrifice.

And so the day came for us to pick up the new car. . . . I still remember the "new car smell" in that Chevy and how it gleamed as we drove it off the lot. But what I'll always be grateful for is that the first thing we did in that car was drive directly to our favorite neighborhood restaurant, forego all our promised scrimping for that glorious day, and feast on burgers and fried chicken and pie *à la mode*. Not quite "living large" by today's standards. But we'd put away the coffee spoons for another day—the cautious, skimpy measure T. S. Eliot describes in "The Love Song of J. Alfred Prufrock": "I have measured out my life in coffee spoons."

WHILE WORKING FOR AN ORGANIZATION THAT DELIVERS LUNCHES TO ELDERLY SHUT-INS, I USED TO TAKE MY FOUR-YEAR-OLD DAUGHTER ON AFTERNOON ROUNDS. SHE WAS INTRIGUED BY THE VARIOUS APPLIANCES OF OLD AGE, PARTICULARLY CANES, WALKERS, AND WHEELCHAIRS. ONE DAY I FOUND HER STARING AT A PAIR OF FALSE TEETH SOAKING IN A GLASS. AS I BRACED FOR THE INEVITABLE QUESTIONS, SHE MERELY WHISPERED, "THE TOOTH FAIRY WILL NEVER BELIEVE THIS!"

Anonymous

Lighten Up

- Remember back to your childhood. Did you ever get a snow day? How did you react? If you have always lived in a climate without snow, remember a time that was equally liberating, like the first day of summer vacation or Christmas break, or a day when the school closed because of a power outage. How does that memory affect your relationship with your children? How might it help you share their delight in a surprise, their heady freedom when the routine changes?

- Read all or part of a book on Sabbath: for instance Wayne Muller's *Sabbath* or Donna Schaper's *Sabbath Keeping*. Try some of their ideas, adapted to your family's lifestyle.

- For a whole week, deliberately build a "snow-break" or "little Sabbath" into everyone's day. Maybe it's just a half-hour in the afternoon or before bed, but make sure there's a little pause for silence or the outdoors. At the end of the week, sum up the experience: What difference did it make to your state of mind? Your happiness? Your relationship with your children?

- Rent a funny video or get some books from the humor section of the library. Turn to these after a stressful day or week.

- Develop a storehouse of funny stories, cartoons that tickle you, and jokes that start you laughing. Each day share one funny treasure with your children, your mate, your co-workers—anyone. Keep your sense of humor alive and well for their own good and your own good.

- At the end of each day, ask your child: What are you grateful for today? What were some of the nice things that happened today? In hints too broad to miss, make sure that he or she asks you the same. Swap blessings of the day. Talking about funny or positive things will help your child and you sleep better and plant seeds of blessing and hope in your spirit.

MY OWN HEART LET ME MORE

HAVE PITY ON; LET

ME LIVE TO MY SAD SELF

HEREAFTER KIND.

Gerard Manley Hopkins

Wedding Dance

---

*W*e are fam . . . i . . . lee the music begins and we tumble onto the dance floor: cousins, aunts, uncles, siblings, grandparents, and a few folks so distantly related no one remembers where they fit on the family tree. It doesn't matter. After a long church wedding, we're ready to dance. We've sat still long enough: through the service, the photos, and the dinner. Now it's time to move, no matter how graceless the steps or how stiff the motions. The dance becomes an intergenerational mix of twist and waltz, hip-hop, and jitterbug.

As I dance in a circle with my four kids and a few cousins, I peek at a variety of steps surrounding us. My cousin's two sons clown around in the exaggerated ballroom style of nine-year-old boys. The bride dances with her sister's three-month-old baby in her arms. A college-aged niece shows her high school brother the latest spin. An aunt and uncle married twenty-five years dance into memory. A misty-eyed grandma, newly widowed, box-steps with a kind and handsome son. We've left behind our high-heeled shoes and tuxedo jackets; now is the time to relax in comfort.

After nagging all week to get the kids' shoes polished and my daughter's bridesmaid dress fitted, I can ease into appreciation, the stress forgotten. I delight in the slender grace of young dancers, the pure energy of little boys' gymnastics. For one brief evening, everyone looks beautiful; everyone smells good; everyone gets along. The wedding captures a snapshot of my extended family at its finest.

Videos of the couples' lives run against one wall of the reception hall. The capsulized history of one young woman and one young man tells a story most of us know only in part. It isn't all the cheery fun of this day. In one shot, holding his first grandchild, is my uncle, the bride's grandpa, who recently died. For many, it's a bittersweet blend to see him so happy then and miss him so much now. There's another shot of the groom's twin brother, killed at age twenty in a car accident, and one of the bride's father, divorced from her mother because of his alcoholism.

At tables around the dance floor, the theme continues: good people endure tough things. My great aunt who tells zany jokes that keep her whole table laughing has suffered through the death of her husband, the schizophrenia of her son, and the birth of two grandchildren whose parents aren't married. Another couple tries not to think now about the unpaid bills and the threat of job termination. Instead they mug for the cameras on each table, tease each other, eat mints, nuts, and wedding cake. A "little sister" drags a "big brother" into line for a picture. She's seventy-seven, and he's eighty-nine.

The conversations do more than fill the spaces between music. Through them, some people connect after twenty years, wonder how they ever grew so far apart. Others who live at opposite ends of the country plan to meet soon—and whether they do isn't the point. The message is, we inhabit the same family mesh. When we explore our lineage, we find out who we are. No longer exiles on this earth, we belong snugly to the place idealized by the theme song from the TV show *Cheers* where "everybody knows your name."

And in casual, unconscious ways, we transmit this sense of belonging to our daughters and sons. Relatives tell the kids funny stories of their parents as children, how my cousin Bill and I could never sit next to each other at dinner because we got in so much trouble together. We admire a girl's curly hair because it reminds us of her mother's, compliment a son who's inherited his dad's sense of humor. We stand squarely in a channel of affection passed down the generations, and do our part to continue the flow.

A child washed by this affirmation shouldn't need to ask "Who am I?" Their identity is mysteriously shaped by soft laps and big hugs, hearty laughter and affirmation. At the moment they may be more interested in leapfrog, or who can burp loudest. But those who can some day excavate memory for these deep sources can eventually become more creative and critical individuals. Those on the fringe of family will lack the easy give-and-take, argument and compliment that occurs in such intimacy.

The marriage ritual we witnessed unites two individuals and creates a new family. It also allows a lot of us to remember who we are and delight in that identity. Our families may annoy us or drive us mad at times, but despite the frustration, few people would trade them in. As crazy and dysfunctional as they may be, they are ours. So we whose task now is to shape children in new families are heartened and inspired by the wedding dance. We hum as we leave the reception and go out into the night.

ATTENDING A WEDDING FOR THE FIRST TIME, A LITTLE GIRL WHISPERED TO HER MOTHER, "WHY IS THE BRIDE DRESSED IN WHITE?"

"BECAUSE WHITE IS THE COLOR OF HAPPINESS, AND TODAY IS THE HAPPIEST DAY OF HER LIFE," THE MOTHER REPLIED, TRYING TO KEEP IT SIMPLE.

THE CHILD THOUGHT ABOUT THIS FOR A MOMENT, THEN ASKED, "SO WHY'S THE GROOM WEARING BLACK?"

Anonymous

Lightening Up and Liberation

No other phrase sends joy into the hearts of both children and adults in wintry climates like the jubilant cry, "Snow Day!" echoing through the house. While it has overtones similar to "Free Ice Cream!" or "Case Dismissed," it opens a unique world.

It introduces the liberation of knowing that the whole world has shut down—airports, schools, factories, banks, offices, sometimes even the government. Our hard, fast commitments suddenly soften. My kids turn their beds into trampolines, jumping up and down with special glee if the spelling test is postponed.

Falling snow has a peaceful, calming effect, as does knowing that I can put everything on hold—pressing phone calls can wait, work can be done tomorrow, the world won't end if I don't answer e-mail. The holiday is delicious if the lunches are packed, the mail is ready to send, and the clothes clean. But it's even better if it means a reprieve from jobs undone: an extra day to prepare the unfinished project. As the children make hot chocolate, start a fire, pull out the sled, or snuggle back into sleep, I reflect on this rare gift of time.

This unexpected release from all that holds us bound says that while the deadline, the clock, the time allocation sheet are part of our responsibilities, they're not the whole story. We were made for more, we are larger than the net of obligations. In the hush of snow sometimes comes time to reflect.

Though the surprise is impossible to recreate, at another level, we can arrange for ourselves a snow day at any time. In the Hebrew tradition, the Sabbath was one day a week when everything stopped. On that day, Beatrice Bruteau says, "Time is suspended and we live in eternity." In his book *Sabbath*, Wayne Muller points out that the traditional cessation of work challenges our workaholic ways. "Our culture enshrines progress: We must always be busy and never rest. If we're not jittery with caffeine, on the move, contributing to the GNP, we're somehow suspect."

But Muller asks: "What if we are not going anywhere? What if we are simply living and growing within an ever-deepening cycle of rhythms, perhaps getting wise, perhaps learning to be kind, and hopefully passing whatever we have learned to our children? . . . Sabbath challenges the theology of progress by reminding us that we are already and always on sacred ground." We can rest in the divine because we don't need to go anywhere; we are already home.

Even those who aren't Jewish and don't traditionally honor the Sabbath can adapt the custom to fit their own lifestyles. When my children were younger, I insisted on a daily naptime to give us a break from each other and restore my sanity. As they grew older, naptime became "quiet time," when everyone in the household retired to privacy and inner resources. This may seem idealistic, but it helps children to develop an inner strength that will serve them later in life. If they can turn to a book, a journal, a musical instrument, a hobby, or a drawing pad, they will rarely be bored anywhere in the world.

Parents should use this daily pause for themselves: not as a chance to catch up on phone calls, laundry, or house cleaning. This is a well-deserved time for the "3 Rs": reflect, rest, read. Through such activities, we renew our links to the deep energy sources: God's vitality within us, our Creator's potency and joy. Parenting is too big a job to leave to tired, limited human resources. It demands that we get in touch with the larger forces that propel the cosmos and drive all human achievement.

Children's voices jolt me out of reverie. It's time to make hot stew in the crockpot. I don't mind the noisy kitchen now because I've had serenity and restoration in the quiet softening of snow.

WHY, ONE BABY IS JUST A HOUSE AND A FRONT YARD FULL BY ITSELF.

Mark Twain

9

Sow Seeds for a Hopeful Future

IT AIN'T OVER 'TIL IT'S OVER.

Yogi Berra

While Yogi Berra was probably referring to a baseball game, he could've been describing parenting as well. It's a game that never stops. At the times we want to exit the ballpark, there are the kids: our children's insistent presence demands our highest loyalty. In a lifetime we may switch careers, move across the country, live in various houses, and have different friends. But parenting is one game we play for good.

The advantage of such a long-range commitment is the chance to hang in there through the failures and stay around long enough for some successes. But it's also fair to say that many parents who try to do the right things have enormous heartaches over their children. Perhaps the only realistic way to look at this huge expenditure of time, money, energy, and talent is as sowing seed.

"How long have I been with you," Jesus once asked his followers, "and still you don't get it?" A parental note crept into the tone of his voice there. And the parental voice reappears when Jesus says, "You do not know now what I am doing, but later you will understand."

I was down on my knees when I began to understand that line of the gospel. Don't assume I was praying. Instead I was looking in the back corner of the bottom kitchen cabinet for the lid to a little recycled cream cheese dish. My daughter likes tomato slices on her sandwiches, but she doesn't like them leaking. So the plastic containers are the perfect solution for packing lunch; she slips the tomato into her sandwich on the spot. Somewhere in the dark recesses of the cabinet lurks a little lid, but that night I couldn't find it. I was edging into the familiar lament, "Why am I doing this?"

In answer I found a glimmer of understanding. The futile hunt for the lid, the laundry sloshing noisily at 9 p.m. so my son could have clean jeans tomorrow, the muffins baking for the office potluck were part of a larger picture—the hopeful "cloud of witnesses" to the sacred ministry of parenting. Somehow I was connected to a monk in Georgia, James Behrens, who had written a meditation as he sat behind a barn. "I want to risk taking God to heart," Behrens wrote, ". . . and later I will know what I do not know now."

The way he takes God to heart is different from the way I do. The monk's job is to sit behind the barn and enter quiet solitude. He approaches things from the contemplative stance, which holds experiences like jewels in the palm, turning them in the light. Then he takes what he learns in stillness and hones it to the cleanest expression he can craft. That might take many rewrites and a lot more work than he ever dreamed he was getting into.

But it's not that different from parenting. I might envy the quiet contemplation, but my lid-hunt or last-minute laundry are different faces of the same quest. We both go beyond the call of duty, mining all we can from an experience. Some people would call it dysfunctional or codependent. But every superb artist and every powerful writer puts in the extra hours, does one more revision, adds the final polishing touch. Or in my case, carefully wraps the leaky tomatoes.

Sure, we could be snoozing happily or even propped in bed with a good book. But folks all over the place are going the extra step. I think gratefully of phone conversations this week with a customer service representative for my health insurance company. I know, most folks cringe at the thought of hours poured into voice mail and a bureaucratic nightmare. But this guy put in extra time to make sure that my son away at college got his broken finger fixed.

Do all our extra efforts "risk taking God to heart"? Maybe not consciously, but the quest for God is tied to the entry deep into our experience.

Much as we yearn for a formal answer to the formal invitation we call prayer, we may instead find God in the doing of things, when we are unconscious of "religion."

So Jesus prayed, and his words, "You do not know now what I am doing, but later you will understand," come as he is on his hands and knees washing the feet of his disciples. Poised on the eve of his death, Jesus does not go off in seclusion to a retreat center nor meditate at the synagogue. He's in the midst of the dinner commotion. John positions his action during supper. It's as hands-on as packing lunches, and seems as unnecessary. The servants could easily wash the feet, and we could probably hand the kids lunch money.

Why does Jesus do the maid's job? He is telling us something about leadership as service, but he is also showing how to live fully and model for the next generation. I like to think of him as telling me, "Go the extra mile—don't just pack the lunch, but write a note to enclose in the lunch sack too, probably signed with a maudlin smiley face."

Another image I appreciate comes from a television commercial, which shows a dad dutifully driving behind his daughter's school bus on her first day of kindergarten. She wants him to "hang around," so he stands guard until she's safely in the classroom door.

Jumping with both feet into whatever experience presents itself not only enriches the doer. It creates a longer memory. The apostle Peter initially protested the foot washing at the last supper, but later came to understand it. Our children may seem oblivious now to much of what we do on their behalf. They may come to understand it later, not through a convoluted thought process, but by doing it themselves.

Take off the cloak, tie a towel around the waist, pour water into a basin, wash some figurative feet. Pack a lunch, do some laundry, make a phone call, probably unaware you're planting seed. Thus begin the spiritual dimensions of parenting.

To MY MIND, THE BEST WAY TO IMPART WISDOM . . . OR ANYTHING ELSE TO YOUR CHILDREN, ESPECIALLY WHEN THEY ARE YOUNG, IS TO LIVE IT YOURSELF, EMBODY WHAT YOU MOST WANT TO IMPART, AND KEEP YOUR MOUTH SHUT.

Jon Kabat-Zinn

Sow Seeds for a Hopeful Future

- Draw a map of your own life, marking the ten events that you see in retrospect were the most important turning points: for instance,

"Grandma's death," "moving to Texas," "promotion to manager." Label those that seemed like beginnings with a B, those that seemed like endings with an E. Are some points hard to label? Look especially at those you might label both B and E. What do they indicate about your own life that might help you guide your child?

- Interview an older person, preferably a grandparent. Ask them how they learned to take life's roller coaster up-and-downs in stride. Or, what do they still struggle with in trying to achieve serenity?

- Spend some time outdoors in the context of "something larger": a natural scene like a lake, a starry sky, a forest, a field, a mountain, or a seashore. How does the vastness of the scene affect your perspective on parenting?

- A mother who knew her cancer was terminal wrote her five-year old daughter a letter to be opened for every major event of her life that the mom knew she would miss. So there was a letter for starting school, first prom, high school graduation, wedding day, birth of the first child, and so on, saying what the mom would like to say if she could be there for the event. As your own conclusion to this book, write each of your children a letter that can be opened now or later on some important day. If you hate to write, make a drawing or a tape recording. Tell them about your hopes and dreams for them, about your love that sometimes in the busy rush of every day doesn't get adequately expressed.

NO SEED EVER SEES THE FLOWER.

Anonymous

Ski Guide

It's a good thing I was wearing sunglasses. I don't like to get caught misty-eyed on a ski slope. It may have been an unusual place for an insight on parenting, but given the background, it makes perfect sense.

Flash back fifteen years to a car full of kids headed toward the mountains. Every inch of space is packed with lunches, jackets, ski boots, poles, skis, backpacks, and goggles—except that we have probably forgotten something vital like one kid's boots. As a friend explained, "Skiing is equipment-intensive."

That wasn't the only intensity. We weren't just out for a fun day, like a normal family. We had set alarms ungodly early for a Saturday morning and were driving pell-mell toward Breckenridge,

Colorado. My younger son was enrolled in ski school there, and lessons started promptly. He was only five, and as I rushed him to class, he looked like a small, bundled polar bear. At least if he fell, he would roll like a well-cushioned potato bug down the mountain.

Either the padding did its job, or he didn't fall much. He was soon skiing like an Olympian, and headed for the hills at every opportunity.

Ironically, his high school would solemnly declare a snow day when the first flake fell, "to protect the students' safety." Little did the principal know that the students took that as their cue to drive further into danger, deeper snow, and a day of skiing.

By the time my son reached college, he went off jumps without blinking and skied double black diamond courses with poise. I bought him a helmet and hoped for the best. Then he volunteered as a guide in the handicapped skier program.

In his first few months, he guided blind people, autistic children, and amputees whose physical limitations didn't stop them from learning to ski. Which brings the story back to Breckenridge, just after lunch. My son had taken his sister for a quick run before he met Robyn, the girl he was guiding that day.

Waiting for them to return, I watched Robyn emerge from the lunchroom to ski that afternoon. She probably had cerebral palsy. Her father manipulated the wheel chair close to the base and waited. I wanted to assure them that my son would soon return, but I had been sworn to anonymity. My role that day was strictly "surreptitious observer."

But as I watched, I couldn't help thinking about the collusion of events that had brought us all there together. Why was that dad pushing the wheel chair, while my son was the able-bodied guide? What mental gifts did Robyn's weakened body hide? This was no easy equation—none of us had earned the roles we were in. We were simply playing out our day in the snow. But one thing became clear: Robyn would not ski that day without my son.

He soon appeared and, with his partner guide, lifted her out of the chair and into a small sled equipped with skis. While these marvelous contraptions are expensive, they enable people with a wide range of disabilities to participate in a sport that might otherwise be impossible. Her dad adjusted her helmet, and Robyn was off. In one smooth movement, my son and his buddy hoisted her sled onto the chairlift. With a grin as broad as the Four O'clock Run, she began ascending the mountain.

I was lucky to glimpse them again at the summit, under the pretext of adjusting my bindings. There, my son steadied the sled and adjusted the ropes that held it to himself. By pulling on either side, he could turn Robyn from right to left and bring her carefully down the mountain. As he bent over her, tethering himself to the sled, his face filled with intense concentration and care. His powerful focus gave new meaning to the old advice, "skiing is equipment-intensive."

I hope Robyn was delighted with her ski adventure. I hope she forgot the fetters of an uncooperative body and soared beyond it for a day. I hope she trusted my son so implicitly that she could savor the scenery whizzing by and the wind across her face. It was clear and cold as the peaks around her brushed the sky. She could be fully a part of the vast white snowscape. Later that day, she probably collapsed exhausted into bed as he did. I hope she dreamed of flying.

The experience defied easy platitudes about being grateful for healthy bodies. Instead, it praised every body. No one spoke of courage. The operative word was "fun." Together we were all caught up in the marvelous poem of creation, and it didn't much matter who was guiding and who was riding. We all breathed the same piney air and gazed on the same magnificent mountains. Somehow, I think we all returned to routine the next day a little achier perhaps, but also a little larger. And mom remembered bundling a five-year old off to ski class, never dreaming where his path would lead.

In every goodbye are the seeds of another hello.

Anonymous

Tragedy and Treasure

The riddle asks, "when is an ending a beginning—or a beginning an end?" Many people know that graduations or marriages can capsulize this ironic twist. But seldom do we turn to the acid test: a tragedy. So it is most dramatic in terrible circumstances, when an end can become a fresh start. While each individual copes with disaster in a unique way, this is the story of how one family handled one of the worst things that could ever happen.

No one could have predicted that when two crazed killers broke into a school library their violent actions could have repercussions across this country and half a world away. That first spray of gunfire would mark the end of one child's life, and a new beginning for another who at the time was not even born.

Tom and Linda Mauser's fifteen-year-old son Daniel was killed as he studied at Columbine High School on April 20, 1999. Their grief led them to establish Project SAFE Colorado, a concerted effort to end gun violence. Many other people agreed with them that the proliferation of guns in the United States was senseless. When state and federal legislatures failed to act, Project SAFE began a one-step-at-a-time program to enact laws protecting the children of Colorado.

The first measure closed the "gun-show loophole," for the first time requiring the same safety procedures and identification for people buying guns at gun shows as a dealer would require in a store. (Ironically, the weapon that killed Daniel was probably purchased at a gun show.) When that ballot initiative passed by a huge majority, it heartened supporters to introduce more legislation, which may eventually make a tremendous difference.

But that is not the only seed that was sown on a tragic day.

Let's shift focus now to the more intimate circle of the Mauser family. A year and a half after Daniel's death, they adopted Madeline, a baby girl from China. Because of government restrictions on family size there, orphanages are teeming with unwanted babies; only two percent of the girls will be adopted. As the Mausers walked through the streets of Nanjing with their older daughter Christine and baby Madeline, people gave them a thumbs-up sign of approval.

Tom theorizes that their support sprang from traditional Chinese reverence for the family. Passers-by guessed that this baby wouldn't be raised in an institution, but brought to a loving home. Knowing nothing of the tragedy in the background, they sent the Mausers back with affirmation. While the family will always miss Daniel, they nevertheless transcended their pain to help a child who would otherwise be homeless. Daniel may have been an innocent victim—but

Madeline wouldn't have to be. She and many others may flourish and bloom in safety.

Asked for parenting advice, Tom shrugs. "Hug your kids," he answers. "A lot."

That is an appropriate note on which to close this book—and begin or continue the real work of parenting. Hug your kids a lot!

BUT IN THAT HOUR LEAST
EXPECTED
WHEN WE ARE MOST OURSELVES
AND NOT DEFLECTED
EVEN BY REMEMBRANCE OF
YOUR NAME,
WE STREAM DOWN THE PATHS
OF GRACE . . .

May Sarton

Notes

Chapter 1

The Search Institute study cited on pages 17-18 is quoted from Peter Benson et al., *What Kids Need to Succeed* (Minneapolis: Free Spirit Publishing, 1998), p. 103.

The Mary Fisher quotation on page 23 is taken in context from William O'Malley, *The Sacraments* (Allen, TX: Tabor, 1995), p. 41.

The May Sarton poem on page 29 is quoted from May Sarton (Bradford Dudley Daziel, ed.), *Sarton Selected: An Anthology of the Journals, Novels, and Poetry of May Sarton* (© May Sarton and Bradley Dudley Daziel, 1989). Used by permission of W. W. Norton & Co., Inc.

Chapter 2

Some of the material in Chapter 2, "Make Your Home a Sacred Space," is reprinted with permission from *Faith Works.*

Chapter 4

The story of family life described as "Hot Potato" on pages 64-65 by Tom McGrath is from Tom's website (www.homefaith.com).

Chapter 5

The context of the story of the Chavez family and noted quotations on pages 82-83 are from "Family Triumphs: Five Kids Harvard Grads" by Jerry Schwartz, AP News, quoted in the *Denver Post* (3 June 2001), p. 27A.

Chapter 6

The activity suggestion on page 105 related to the quotation by Mary Pipher is from Mary Pipher, *The Shelter of Each Other* (New York: Ballantine Books, 1996), p. 244.

Chapter 7

The quotations by Robert McClory on page 118 are quoted from the article "You're Still Worth More Than Many Sparrows," *U.S. Catholic* (September 1996), p. 42.

Chapter 9

The story of the Mausers was originally told in the article "Adopted Baby Brings New Life to Mausers," *Denver Catholic Register* (18 April 2001).

The May Sarton poem on page 157 is quoted from May Sarton (Bradford Dudley Daziel, ed.), *Sarton Selected: An Anthology of the Journals, Novels, and Poetry of May Sarton* (© May Sarton and Bradley Dudley Daziel, 1989). Used by permission of W. W. Norton & Co., Inc.

KATHY COFFEY has written several books, including *Dancing in the Margins, Experiencing God with Your Children*, and *Hidden Women in the Gospels*. She has received several awards for her columns, books, and poetry. Coffey works as an editor and is a frequent speaker at national workshops. She lives in Denver, Colorado with her family.